CITYSPOTS
PALM

Teresa Fisher

Written by Teresa Fisher
Original photography by Teresa Fisher
Front cover photography courtesy of Alamy Images

Produced by 183 Books
Design/layout/maps: Chris Lane and Lee Biggadike, Studio 183 Ltd
Editorial/project management: Stephen York

Published by Thomas Cook Publishing
A division of Thomas Cook Tour Operations Limited
PO Box 227, Units 15/16, Coningsby Road
Peterborough PE3 8SB, United Kingdom
email: books@thomascook.com
www.thomascookpublishing.com
+44 (0)1733 416477

First edition © 2006 Thomas Cook Publishing
Text © 2006 Thomas Cook Publishing
Maps © 2006 Thomas Cook Publishing
ISBN-13: 978-1-84157-550-6
ISBN-10: 1-84157-550-X
Project Editor: Kelly Anne Pipes
Production/DTP: Steven Collins

Printed and bound in Spain by GraphyCems

CONTENTS

SYMBOLS & ABBREVIATIONS

The following symbols are used throughout this book:

☎ telephone   **✆** fax   **✉** email   **⊕** website address
⊙ address   **⊙** opening times   **⊗** public transport connections

The following symbols are used on the maps:

ℹ Tourist Information Office
✈ Airport

Hotels and restaurants are graded by approximate price as follows:
€ budget **€€** mid-range **€€€** expensive

24-HOUR CLOCK

All times in this book are given in the 24-hour clock system used widely in Europe and in most international transport timetables.

◐ *The city of Palma sweeps around its bay and merges with its neighbouring resorts*

Introduction

Palma Town, beautifully situated at the centre of Palma Bay, is the capital of the Balearic Islands. This vibrant, cosmopolitan city has managed to retain a great deal of its ancient charm. Its street life and thriving arts scene lead many people to compare it with the stylish Catalan capital, Barcelona. Indeed, Palma was voted the best place to live in all of Spain in a recent survey by a leading Spanish newspaper – because of its chic shops and avant-garde galleries, its thriving pavement café society, excellent restaurants and lively nightlife and, above all, because of its sheer vitality, and the flair and enthusiasm of its inhabitants.

The most striking image of Palma is its triumphant cathedral, standing proud on the waterfront and almost seeming to grow out of the sea. Fanning out behind the cathedral is the old town and Arab quarter, a warren of narrow lanes shielding ancient palaces and mansions, with elegant courtyards featuring stone stairways and potted plants. A short stroll from here leads to Plaça Major, a pleasant square of open-air cafés, at the heart of the pedestrian shopping district with its many small speciality shops. Amble down leafy La Rambla, with its dozens of flower-sellers, through Plaça Weyler and Plaça del Mercat with their unusual *Modernista* architecture, tree-lined Passeig des Born, the city's main promenade since the early 15th century, and into the narrow maze of streets around La Llotja – venue of some of the smartest hotels, bars and restaurants in town. From here it is a stone's throw to the waterfront, where the real lifeblood of Palma lies. Fishermen mend their nets, cruise ships sail into the harbour, and the designer bars along the Passeig Marítim buzz with conversation after dark.

There's no denying Palma offers both residents and visitors the good life and – with the opening of new shops, galleries, hotels and restaurants – the future looks bright. Long overlooked, it is finally becoming a popular holiday destination in its own right. Easy access makes it perfect for a weekend away. Seek out its many treasures, soak up its cosmopolitan atmosphere, and you will discover the true Palma – laid back, vibrant and one of the most exhilarating cities in Spain.

● The flower-bedecked Rambla is one of the city's most pleasant streets

When to go

CLIMATE

Palma's temperate climate makes it a pleasant city-break destination all year round. However, when planning your holiday you may wish to consider the old Mallorcan saying *Hasta el cuarenta de mayo no te quites el sayo*, meaning 'Don't discard your coat until the 40th day of May' (in other words, until 10 June), which is considered to be the first day of summer.

Most people choose to visit between April and September when the island is invariably warm and sunny. July and August are the hottest months, when temperatures can rise well above 30°C (80–90°F). However, Palma is also popular at other times of the year, and usually more pleasant for a city break outside the sweltering

● *Palma's year-round sunshine is one of its greatest assets*

summer high season. During January and February, the almond blossom makes an unforgettable sight, and Easter is especially popular, with its mild spring days. However, autumn is generally regarded as the best time to visit, when the main tourist rush is over but the sea is still warm enough for bathing and the evenings remain balmy enough for al fresco dining. During the winter, many beach resorts and tourist facilities around the island close down, but Palma continues to attract visitors all year round. Its wettest months are generally October and February. In the depths of winter temperatures in the city can drop as low as 2–3°C (35–37°F), while snow occasionally falls in the mountains in the north of the island.

FIESTAS & FESTIVALS

Fiestas and festivals are an integral part of Mallorcan life. The fiesta calendar is at its busiest between June and September, when scarcely a week goes by without one taking place somewhere on the island.

In Palma, the first event in the annual fiesta calendar is the Fiesta of Sant Antoni, the patron saint of animals (17 January), a colourful parade through the city in which hundreds of riders on horseback and numerous other animals all participate. The biggest fiesta takes place on 20 January, the Fiesta of Sant Sebastià , the patron saint of the city. Many of the squares are transformed into stages for live music to suit all tastes – rock, jazz, flamenco and classical. Palma also hosts the most spectacular Carnival fiesta on the island (just before Lent), known as the Cavalcade (Sa Rua). The inspiration for most festivities is religious, and Semana Santa (Holy Week) plays an especially important part in the city's cultural calendar. Events include the traditional blessing of palms and olive branches at churches on Palm Sunday, and the solemn procession from the church of La Sang, on Maundy Thursday, where the image of the crucified Christ is carried through the city. During summer months, look out for St Peter's Day in June, when the patron saint of

PUBLIC HOLIDAYS

As well as countless local festivals and fiestas, many Spanish national holidays are observed in Palma. The main ones are as follows:

1 Jan New Year's Day

6 Jan Epiphany

19 Mar Sant José (St Joseph's Day)

Mar/Apr Good Friday, Easter Monday

1 May Labour Day

May/June Corpus Christi

24 June Sant Juan (St John's Day – the King's name-day)

29 June Sant Pedro y Sant Pablo (St Peter and St Paul's Day)

25 July Sant Jaume (St James' Day)

15 Aug Assumption of the Virgin

12 Oct National Day

1 Nov Todos los Santos (All Saints' Day)

6 Dec Constitution Day

8 Dec Feast of the Immaculate Conception

25 Dec Christmas Day

On national holidays, most businesses and shops are closed, public transport is reduced to a minimum, and it can be difficult to find accommodation. At Easter and Christmas many shops and offices are closed for longer periods.

fishermen is honoured with processions of fishing boats, and the Dia de Virgen de Carmen (15–16 July), another parade and blessing of fishing boats, this time in honour of the Virgin Mary. On the third Saturday in October, the Fiesta of Santa Catalina Tomas brings further singing, parades and street entertainment. At Christmas, Noche Buena (24 December) is marked with nativity plays and midnight mass services, and Santos Inocentes (28 December) is the Spanish equivalent of April Fool's Day. The final event of the year in Palma is the Festa de l'Estandart (31 December), commemorating the Catalan conquest of the island in 1229.

● *Dramatic firework displays mark the Fiesta of Sant Sebastià*

Palma's art & architecture

Mallorca has long been an artists' haven, thanks to its Mediterranean location, its exotic blend of European and Arab culture, and its beautiful landscapes. Modern art, in particular, has flourished since the start of the 20th century, thanks largely to two men, the great Catalan artist, Joan Miró (1893–1983), and the great Catalan architect, Antoni Gaudí (1852–1926).

ARCHITECTURAL GENIUS

In 1902, a local bishop, having seen Gaudí's flamboyant Sagrada Família church in his home town of Barcelona, invited him to restore Palma's cathedral. Gaudí spent ten years working intermittently on the cathedral, introducing to Palma Europe's latest architectural fashion, *Modernista* or Spanish art nouveau – a trend known to some as *la época de mal gusto* ('the epoch of bad taste'). He made some radical changes to the interior of the cathedral, including the introduction of electric lighting, wrought-iron railings and a highly controversial canopy symbolising the Crown of Thorns, made from cardboard, cork, brocade and nails. Gaudí's influence can be seen in several of Palma's early 20th-century buildings, including Pensió Menorquina and Can Casasayas in Plaça del Mercat with their rippling facades, and Lluis Forteza Rei's lavish masterpiece, Can Rei in Carrer Bolseria, with its mosaic facade and ornate wrought-ironwork.

AN ARTISTIC 'SAINT'

Joan Miró's arrival in Mallorca also boosted artistic creativity throughout the island. Both his mother and wife were Mallorca-born and the great painter and sculptor spent his childhood

🔺 *Elaborate ironwork is a trademark of the Mordernista style*

holidays and the last 40 years of his life living and working on the outskirts of Palma in Cala Major. He once remarked: 'As a child, I loved to watch the always changing Mallorcan sky. At night I would get carried away by the writing in the sky of the shooting stars, and the lights of the fireflies ... It was here that I received the first creative seeds which became my work.' During his time in Mallorca, Miró moved away from realism and developed his own characteristically spontaneous style of bold lines and bright splashes of primary colours. His studio in Cala Major remains almost untouched since his death, as part of the Fundació Pilar i Joan Miró (see page 106), and, to Mallorcans, he is nothing less than a saint.

History

Mallorca abounds in ancient monuments dating back to the earliest traces of civilisation here in 5000BC. From caves to stone-built houses, the Talayotic civilisation followed around 2000BC and, largely due to its strategic location in the Mediterranean, the Balearic Islands soon became important trading posts for Phoenicians, then Greeks and Carthaginians, who used the islands for piracy. At this time, the locals were known for their ability to defend themselves by using slings, hence the archipelago received its name, derived from the Greek word *ballein* meaning 'to throw from a sling'.

Mallorca flourished under the Romans (123BC–AD500), with the introduction of Christianity, vines and olives, and a network of roads and settlements – including two major cities, *Palmaria* (Palma) and *Pollentia* (Pollença). After successive invasions by the Vandals and the Byzantines, the island eventually fell to the Arabs in 902. Moorish culture prevailed for several centuries. Oranges, windmills, new irrigation techniques, almonds and apricots were introduced, and the lifestyle of citizens in Palma (then known as *Medina Mayurqa*) was the envy of Europe, with their heated baths, street lights and covered sewers. This sophistication drew the attention of potential conquerors, and in 1229 the young Catalan king, Jaume I of Aragón, set sail to conquer the 'pirate's nest of Mallorca'. He seized Palma – 'the most beautiful city I have set eyes upon' – on New Year's Eve, and proceeded to replace the mosques with churches and to build the imposing Castell de Bellver. His reign (1229–1276) is still regarded as Mallorca's golden age of independence.

Despite centuries of relentless invasions and conquests, by the start of the 14th century Palma was considered to have one of the most economically successful societies in Christendom. Its merchants' palaces were much admired and the Mallorcan cogs were the best ships on the sea, leading the way in Atlantic exploration. The island's cartographers became celebrated throughout the world. Following a period of political uncertainty in the 16th century, sea trade started to flourish again in the 18th and 19th centuries and, in 1833, a regular ferry service enhanced links between Palma and mainland Spain.

The island's seafaring tradition continued into the early 20th century, bringing visitors by yacht or on cruise ships to Palma. But it wasn't until 1950 with the arrival of the first charter flights that Mallorca witnessed the birth of package tourism. Almost overnight the island became one of Europe's most popular holiday destinations, as greedy developers bulldozed their way along the coast around Palma, eager to cash in on the enormous economic potential of their beaches, in an uncontrolled building boom. Palma, however, has always been more than a developers' playground. In the past five years, it has restored its palaces and museums and shed its image of dusty provincialism. Every week another chic new shop opens, or a boutique hotel, a trendy bar or a minimalist restaurant. Yet at the same time, Palma maintains a careful balance between traditional and modern. Finally this vibrant, cosmopolitan city has now become a popular holiday destination in its own right.

🔺 *Junipero Serra, Mallorcan founder of California*

Lifestyle

The population of Mallorca is 732,000, of whom nearly half live in Palma. The islanders are loyal, friendly and fiercely proud of their identity. They are a largely conformist society, centred on the family and the church – the Catholic Church has held sway here since the Reconquest in 1229. Mealtimes are an especially important occasion, when friends and family gather together. Mallorcans love to spend time over their dinner. They enjoy good lively conversation and never rush their food. They eat hugely but always drink in moderation – unlike many of the foreign visitors holidaying on the island, you never see an islander drunk.

The pace of life in Palma is lively compared with the rural interior. The city is the economic, political and commercial capital of the island, and although the Palmesanos work hard, they play hard too. Office hours (typically 08.00–13.00 and 16.00–19.00) fit neatly

⬥ *Modern Palma still has a traditional fishing fleet*

WHAT'S IN A NAME?

The Palmesanos refer to Palma simply as Ciutat ('City') – a reference to its first name, Civitas (Latin for 'city'), given by the Romans who also called the city Palmaria. It wasn't until the 16th century that it became called Palma – a shortened version of the Roman name. In between, it became known as Medin (Arab for 'city'), and later, when the Christians seized the city, it was called Ciutat de Mallorca.

round a lengthy afternoon siesta, giving locals the energy to party late into the night. For a true taste of Palma, chat to locals over early-morning coffee and *ensaimadas* (sweet pastries) in a simple café; shop till you drop with the smart set in Avinguda Sant Jaume III – the cost of living is generally higher in Palma than elsewhere on the island; then join in their evening *paseo* (a ritual evening stroll when all the family parade their best clothes) down the Born and along Passeig Marítim as the sun sets over the Bay of Palma.

Visitors to Palma will hear a variety of languages in the streets – many of its inhabitants are foreigners, especially during summer months. Most Mallorcans are bilingual, speaking both Castilian Spanish and a local version of Catalan known as Mallorquín. During the Franco regime, Mallorquín was banned, but it is once again recognised and can be heard throughout the island, although Catalan is acknowledged as the 'official' language. Numerous ex-pats live in the city, and so British and other foreign-language newspapers and magazines can be bought from newsagents in the city centre and in some of the larger resorts, including the popular English-language newspaper *Majorca Daily Bulletin*, affectionately known as 'The Daily Bee'.

Culture

For centuries, Palma has been the main cultural hub of the Balearic Islands, famed for its enormous number of outstanding buildings, monuments and art galleries. However, in recent years, its reputation has stretched further afield and it is now considered to be an important Mediterranean cultural centre, known particularly for its modern art and its prestigious musical events.

Visitors to Palma can enjoy concerts and music festivals throughout the year, including a festival of classical and light music for the Sant Sebastià fiesta in January, an international week of organ music in March, a spring opera season from March to June at the Teatre Principal, a series of 'summer serenades' in the Castell de Bellver throughout July and August as well as festivals of open-air concerts and recitals, various jazz events throughout the summer months, and a week of organ concerts in October. Then there is a winter opera season, and a winter series of concerts by the Ciutat de Palma Symphony Orchestra.

Palma wears its history on its sleeve, with its eclectic mix of architecture. The historic buildings of Palma bear witness to over a thousand years of history, from the Royal Palace of Almudaina, built by Muslim rulers and remodelled by Christian kings, to La Seu – one of the world's finest Gothic cathedrals – and the city's immaculately restored merchants' palaces of the 15th and 16th century. Some of these palaces are still owned by the descendants of the wealthy patricians who built them, and occasionally they open their doors to the public, providing a rare glimpse of bygone life during Palma's maritime heyday. Otherwise, the city's fascinating museums leave

▶ *Try making up a name for this sculpture at the Fundació Miró*

no stone unturned, documenting city life and local cultural activity over the centuries, ranging from the ancient remains of the Arab Baths to the ultra-modern new gallery, Es Baluard – a cornucopia of glass, metal and brick, built inside an ancient city fortress overlooking the Bay of Palma, with its dazzling collection of 20th- and 21st-century modern art and sculpture.

Mallorca has long attracted painters and there are more than fifty private galleries in Palma that exhibit works mainly by Mallorcan and Catalan artists. Several hold regular free exhibitions of contemporary art, ranging from conventional landscape scenes to avant-garde abstract works by such leading local exponents as Miquel Barcelo. The island's public foundations also help to promote local culture, funding free exhibitions of visual arts in such venues as Fundación la Caixa, Can Solleric, Sa Llotja and Fundación March. Art appreciation is currently in vogue in Palma, and a handful of galleries have recently opened cafés, bars and bookshops on their premises to attract a wider audience.

Tourists, too, can really get to know and love this culturally rich city by participating in the popular series of daytime guided walks on such themes as 'The City and the Sea', 'Modernism in Palma', Monumental Palma, The Jewish Quarter and, an evening stroll entitled 'The Stories and Legends of Palma'. Contact the tourist office (see page 153) or ☎ 971 720720 for information.

Portals Nous is one of Palma's most fashionable beach areas

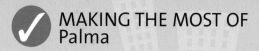

MAKING THE MOST OF
Palma

Shopping

Palma is without doubt the best place to shop in Mallorca. The main shopping district lies within the old city walls and can easily be explored on foot. As Palma's confidence has grown over the past few years, so has its shopping scene increased (and, regrettably, its prices). Growing numbers of chic boutiques and design shops have opened in the city centre – taking their lead from their trendy Catalan neighbour, Barcelona, less than four hours away by ferry – putting Palma on the map for even the most indefatigable shopaholic.

Serious shoppers should head for Avinguda Jaume III, long considered the city's most exclusive shopping boulevard, lined with designer boutiques, and Palma's main branch of Spain's leading department store, El Corte Ingles. Those who enjoy browsing in small, specialist shops should make for the area around Plaça Major. Carrer de Jaume II and pedestrianised Carrer de Sant Miquel are good for reasonably priced boutiques, Carrer de Sindicat abounds with shoe shops, and Carrer de l'Argentería is best for jewellery – look out for Majorica pearls.

Some of the most fascinating shops are hidden away in the narrow streets and alleyways of the old town, where you can find such genuine Mallorcan articles as carved olive-wood, hand-blown glass and glazed earthenware pots painted with the Spanish symbols of cockerels or flowers. Look out also for clay whistles (*siurell*) in the shape of a man on a donkey, rope-soled espadrilles, and authentic lace and cotton decorated with the traditional Mallorcan *llengua* (tongue) pattern.

For self-catering visitors, there is an excellent choice of well-stocked supermarkets but, for fresh produce, you can't beat the Olivat market hall (near Plaça d'Espanya, open every morning except

Sunday) for fruit, vegetables, meat and cheese. A big *rastrillo* (flea market) takes place on Saturday mornings in Avinguda Villalonga.

Most shops open Monday to Friday from 09.00 or 10.00 until 13.00, when they close in the afternoon for a siesta, reopening around 16.30 until 20.00 or even later during summer months. On Saturdays, shops only open in the morning. However, hypermarkets stay open all day, and El Corte Inglés (see pages 90 and 108) is open Monday to Saturday from 10.00 until 22.00.

USEFUL SHOPPING PHRASES

What time do the shops open/close?
¿A qué hora abren/cierran las tiendas?
¿A kay ora abren/theeyerran las teeyendas?

How much is this?
¿Cuánto es?
¿Cwantoe es?

Can I try this on?
¿Puedo probarme esto?
¿Pwedo probarme esto?

My size is ...
Mi número es el ...
Mee noomero es el ...

I'll take this one, thank you
Me llevo éste
Meh llievo esteh

This is too large/too small/too expensive. Do you have any others?
Es muy grande/muy pequeño/muy caro. ¿Tienen más?
Es mooy grandeh/mooy pekenio/mooy karo. ¿Teeyenen mas?

Eating & drinking

Palma's impressive range of restaurants suits every taste and budget from pizza to paella, and from gourmet cuisine to Chinese takeaway. The growth in tourism over the past few decades has led to an increasing number of international restaurants in Palma. Traditional Mallorcan cuisine, however, is typically Mediterranean, making full use of local produce – especially pork, fish and vegetables – all heavily flavoured with garlic, tomato and herbs.

Most meals start with bread and olives (often the tart green olives typical of the island), followed by fresh leafy salads in summer and hearty broths for chilly winter days. Popular local dishes include *frit mallorquí*, a fry-up of liver, potatoes and tomatoes, and *sopes mallorquines*, a thick vegetable soup containing slices of brown bread, as well as the delicious *tumbet*, a ratatouille of potatoes, peppers and aubergines. The Mallorcans are hearty meat-eaters – charcoal grills are a speciality, along with roast suckling pig and shoulder of lamb. *Sobrasada* sausages, made by mincing raw pork with hot red peppers, can be seen hanging in butcher's shops and

RESTAURANT CATEGORIES

In this book the approximate price bands into which restaurants fall are based on the average cost of a three-course evening meal for one person, excluding drinks, indicated by these symbols:

€€€ Over €40; €€ €25–40; € €25 or under.

Bear in mind that a one-course lunch in a €€€ establishment may well be at a €€ cost, and so on.

🔺 *A Mallorcan lunch can be a serious affair spread over several hours*

tapas bars, along with whole cured hams. Seafood features on most menus and there is a glut of fish restaurants, especially on the waterfront. Lobster, prawns and sardines are always excellent, and sea bass baked in rock salt is an island speciality.

The classic Spanish dish is, of course, paella – a mound of steaming rice flavoured with saffron and topped with everything from mussels and prawns to pieces of chicken. The Mallorcan equivalent is *arròs brut* ('dirty rice'), which uses chicken and pork but no seafood. Paella is available in all of Palma's fish restaurants and in many of the resorts, but be wary of anyone who says they can serve it immediately – if cooked properly it takes at least 20 minutes to produce.

Tapas bars abound in Palma, and the area around Plaça Llotja is especially popular. These Spanish nibbles are designed to whet the appetite before a meal, but order enough of them and it can make a meal in itself. They are usually lined up in a display cabinet beneath the bar in metal trays, so it is easy to choose what you want by pointing. Typical tapas range from plates of ham, cheese and olives to more exotic offerings such as fried squid rings, garlic snails, stuffed peppers and meatballs in tomato sauce.

For a simple lunchtime snack try *pa amb oli*, an open sandwich consisting of thick brown bread rubbed with tomato and olive oil, and topped with ham or cheese. Another popular snack is *tortilla*, a delicious potato omelette which is sometimes served cold. Most bars serve *bocadillos* (filled rolls), and bakeries are a good place for stocking up on picnic provisions. Look out for *coca* (a kind of thin Mallorcan pizza), *empanadas* (small pasties filled with meat, fish or spinach) and *ensaimadas* (spiral-shaped pastries that can be either savoury or sweet). Add cheese, fruit and vegetables from the covered market, Mercat Oliva (open every morning except Sunday), and your picnic is ready to enjoy in a city park or at the beach.

The *vin de la casa* (house wine) in most restaurants will probably be Mallorcan and is certainly worth a try. For something a bit more special, order a bottle of wine from mainland Spain. Cava, or Spanish champagne, makes an inexpensive treat and is sometimes combined with fruit juices for a refreshing cocktail. Beer (*cerveza*) is usually lager, sold draught or bottled. (If you want draught, ask for *una cana*.) Sherry, served dry (*fino*) and chilled, is the perfect drink to accompany a plate of ham before a meal. Another refreshing drink is *sangria*, an alcoholic fruit punch based on red wine, brandy and lemonade – delicious, but beware, it's more potent than it tastes. Most bars stock a good selection of Spanish brandies – popular brands include Soberano and Fundador – but for a truly local drink try *hierbas*, a herb-based Mallorcan liqueur which comes either sweet or dry.

Most Mallorcans eat their main meal at lunchtime, and tend to eat dinner late in the evening. Some restaurants do not take reservations, but in summer it's advisable to book for dinner if possible, especially if you're planning to eat in an expensive or popular restaurant. At the end of the meal, it is normal to leave a tip of 10 per cent, assuming service is not included.

USEFUL DINING PHRASES

I would like a table for ... people
Quisiera una mesa para ... personas
Keyseeyera oona mesa para ... personas

May I have the bill, please?
¿Podría traerme la cuenta¡ por favor?
¿Pordreea trayerme la cwenta por farbor?

Waiter/waitress!
Camarero/Camarera!
¡Camareroe/Camarera!

Could I have it well-cooked/medium/rare please?
¿Por favor, la carne bien cocida/al punto/roja?
¿Porr fabor, la kahrrne beeyen kotheeda/al poontoh/roha?

I am a vegetarian. Does this contain meat?
Soy vegetariano. ¿Tiene carne este plato?
Soy begetahreeahnoh. ¿Teeyene carneh esteh plahtoh?

Where is the toilet (restroom) please?
¿Dónde están los servicios, por favor?
¿Donde estan los serbeetheeos, por fabor?

Entertainment & nightlife

Palmesanos certainly know how to enjoy their evening entertainment and nightlife. Indeed, local artist Santiago Rusinyol once famously remarked, 'The people of Palma take the moon as others take the sun'. It's true – Palma is a city that never sleeps. A typical evening might begin with tapas in a local bar after work with friends or colleagues, followed by dinner late in the evening. Theatre performances rarely start before 22.00, cinemas frequently have late-night showings, and the pavement terraces of bars and cafés are usually bustling with activity well into the early hours on summer evenings, while the nightclubs party till dawn.

Palma boasts Mallorca's widest range of entertainment, attracting world-class performers year round. On the cultural front, there are three main theatre venues staging everything from classical to contemporary drama (most performances are in Spanish) as well as dance, ballet, classical concerts, opera and *zarzuela* (Spanish light opera). There are also several cinema complexes in the city, showing mostly 'original version' movies subtitled in Castilian Spanish. Programmes are advertised in the local newspapers. Each venue has its own box office.

Perhaps the most popular evening pastime, however, is people-watching at a pavement terrace, whilst sipping a chilled beer, a bottle of local wine or a *café con hielo* (coffee with ice) with friends. The main core of the city's nightlife is in the city centre, along the waterfront and especially in the maze of ancient side streets behind Plaça Llotja. Here you will find bars to suit all tastes, budgets and ages from trendy neon-lit cocktail bars, to more traditional-style cafés, even pubs and dark smoky blues bars, some of which stay open until dawn.

There is also a wide variety of live music, from mellow jazz to flamboyant displays of authentic *flamenco sevillanas* and *rocieros* dancing, or simply just a good old singsong in an Irish bar. Near the cathedral, Ses Voltes in the Parc de la Mar is a popular open-air venue for live pop, rock or jazz bands most weekends. The city also has a vibrant busking scene, from classical musicians performing around the cathedral square, to human 'statues', clowns and folk bands along La Rambla and the Passeig des Born.

After midnight, night owls should head west along the Passeig Marítim for the currently 'in' late-night bars on the Darsena de Ca'n Barbara, before rubbing shoulders with the likes of the Crown Prince of Spain, Michael Douglas and Claudia Schiffer in the hippest nightclubs in town. There are plenty of clubs to choose from, with DJs playing everything from house and hip-hop to chart sounds and Latin beats.

Although Palma's nightlife is thriving, it is currently fashionable for Palma's chic set to head out of town to the sophisticated bars of nearby Porto Portals, Mallorca's very own St Tropez, a short distance along the coast to the west, or to the smart new waterfront bars and cafés of Portixol, a trendy suburb to the east of Palma.

To find out what's on when, check out the listings on the Tourist Office's official website www.infomallorca.net, or pick up a *Mallorca Week* events sheet produced in English from the Tourist Office. The English-language newspaper, the *Majorca Daily Bulletin* (available at most news kiosks and online at www.majorcadailybulletin.es), provides a daily guide to what's on in the Balearics. There is also a free monthly island guide in English called *Digame*, detailing Mallorcan cinema, theatre, art, music and nightlife available in selected bars and cafés and hotels (and online at www.digame-online.com).

Sport & relaxation

SPECTATOR SPORTS

Mallorcans are football crazy, and the island's two main teams –
Real Mallorca and Atlético Baleares – are both based in Palma, with
regular matches from September to April. Their matches are always
great fun to attend. Ask the tourist office how best to get tickets.

Horse-racing is another great family day out. The sport has been
popular here for over 200 years, ever since neighbouring villages
used to race each other during fiestas. Trotting races take place
every Sunday at the Son Pardo Hippodrome (ⓐ Carretera Palma-
Sóller, km 3. ⓣ 971 754031. ⓦ www.hipodromsonpardo.com).
Bullfighting in Palma is not as popular as in mainland Spain but, if
you wish to view this controversial sport, the city's bullring is the
third largest in Spain and holds fights on selective Sundays between
March and October. ⓐ Plaça de Toros, Avinguda Gaspar B Arquitecte
32. ⓣ 971 755245.

Sailing is a spectacular spectator sport, with regattas in Palma
Bay including the Princess Sofia Trophy in April and the Copa del Rey
in August – both major international yachting events patronised by
King Juan Carlos.

PARTICIPATION SPORTS

The range of participatory sports available in Palma is wide and the
facilities generally excellent. Watersports are hugely popular on the
island, with small boats, canoes and pedalos for hire on an hourly
basis on the Platja de Palma (Palma Beach) at Can Pastilla and
S'Arenal. There is a scuba-diving club in Palma (ⓐ Carrer Roger de
Llúria 4. ⓣ 971 740943) and jetski hire from the Club Náutico at
S'Arenal from June to September (ⓣ 678 652080). For details on

water-skiing, contact the Escuela Esquí Náutico (ⓔ Carrer D. Rafael Pablo. ⓣ 971 230328).

In recent years, golf has boomed on the island. The best of Mallorca's 18 courses are just a stone's throw from Palma, and include Real Golf de Bendinat (ⓣ 971 405200) near Illetas, and Golf Son Muntana (ⓣ 971 783030) and the exclusive Son Vida (ⓣ 971 791120), located just north-west of the city in a lush area of countryside known as S'Hort de Palma (the Garden of Palma).

Walkers, cyclists and nature lovers should leave the city and head for the mountains, where the huge variety of terrain and the abundance of flora and fauna are sure to delight. To scale the big peaks, it is best to join a guided trek organised by the Federacíon Española de Montanismo in Palma (ⓣ 971 468807).

🔺 *Palma has plenty to offer divers*

Accommodation

Palma offers visitors an excellent choice of accommodation, with over 50 hotels ranging from top-class international chains and ultra-chic boutique hotels to simple hotels and inexpensive hostels for travellers on a budget. Surprisingly, there are no campsites on Mallorca.

Hotels are classified by government inspectors with a star system that goes from the basic one-star to five-star luxury. Prices are regulated by the tourist authorities and breakfast is usually not included, unless you are on a package holiday. Tariffs are displayed at the reception desk and in individual rooms. A tax of 7 per cent (rising to 15 per cent in five-star hotels) may or may not be included in the quoted price of your hotel, so it is always advisable to ask prior to booking. The amount is always specified on the rate card.

If you are without transport, stay in the heart of the city, in a converted palace in one of the narrow streets of the medieval centre, or in the alleys behind Plaça Llotja, where the bulk of Palma's budget accommodation can be found, as well as some of its fanciest boutique hotels. For a room with a view, consider a hotel on the Passeig Marítim overlooking the harbour, and, for unadulterated luxury, choose one of the five-star deluxe hotels on the outskirts of the city.

> **PRICE RATING**
> The ratings below (unrelated to the official star system) indicate the approximate cost of a room for two people for one night (excluding VAT and breakfast):
> **€€€** Upwards of €200; **€€** €100–200; **€** Under €100.

Wherever you stay, early booking is essential, especially during high season. You are unlikely to find vacancies by simply walking around the city. It is always advisable to book in advance, either directly with the hotel or through a central booking system, the Central de Reservas de la Federación Empressaria Hotelera de Mallorca (FEHM) ☎ 971 706007; 🖥 www.mallorcahotelguide.com

HOTELS

Almudaina € A moderately sized three-star hotel in the city centre, on Palma's fashionable main shopping precinct. Ask for a room with a view over the rooftops to Palma Bay. 📍 Avda. Jaime III 9.
☎ 971 727340; 🖥 www.hotelalmudaina.com

Born € This former 16th-century *palacio* in the old city, with its classic courtyard entrance with palm trees and marble floors, has been characterfully converted into a simple, comfortable two-star hotel. 📍 Carrer Sant Jaume 3. ☎ 971 712942.

Palladium € Centrally located, near Es Baluard – the new contemporary art museum – and a short walk from the old town, this comfortable three-star hotel is a popular business choice.
📍 Passeig de Mallorca 40. ☎ 971 712 841;
🖥 www.hotelpalladium.com

Pons € A simple one-star hotel in a beautiful old house, with rooms arranged around a central courtyard. 📍 Carrer Vi 8. ☎ 971 722658.

Ritzi € The clean, simple rooms in this popular one-star hotel are ideal for the budget-conscious traveller. Some rooms have shared bath or shower facilities. 📍 Carrer Apuntadores 6. ☎ 971 714610.

Costa Azul €€ This high-rise hotel on the seafront is centrally located and is excellent value, if a little noisy. There is a swimming pool and each room has its own balcony overlooking the bay.
ⓐ Passeig Marítim 7. ① 971 731940 Ⓦ www.fehm.es/pmi/costa

Dalt Murada €€ A stylish, family-owned 15th-century town house with tapestries and chandeliers, in a deserted backstreet near the cathedral: fourteen rooms are arranged around a sunny courtyard of orange and lemon trees. ⓐ Carrer Almudaina 6a. ① 971 425300; Ⓦ www.daltmurada.com

Palau Sa Font €€ Just off the Passeig Marítim and near the main nightlife area, this charming 16th-century episcopal palace has recently been transformed into a small, bijou hotel, combining traditional materials with modern Mediterranean decor.
ⓐ Carrer Apuntadores 38. ① 971 712277; Ⓦ www.palausafont.com

Portixol €€ This sophisticated seafront hotel, a 10-minute walk from the city centre on the revamped Portixol Marina, has a fashionably uncluttered interior and caters to a young jetset crowd.
ⓐ Carrer Sirena 27. ① 971 271800; Ⓦ www.portixol.com

San Lorenzo €€ An elegant baroque mansion full of Mallorcan character in the old fishing quarter, with just six rooms, a picturesque garden and an outdoor pool. ⓐ Carrer San Lorenzo 14.
① 971 728200; Ⓦ www.hotelsanlorenzo.com

▶ *The Palau Sa Font was once the bishop's residence*

Tres €€ One of the latest boutique hotels to open in Palma, this hip Swedish-owned hotel in the old town has 41 comfortable, designer rooms, a beautiful courtyard, a sauna and a rooftop terrace with breathtaking views of the cathedral. ⓐ Carrer Apuntadores 3. ❶ 971 717333; Ⓦ www.hoteltres.com

Arabella €€€ Arguably the island's most luxurious hotel, with its own Michelin-starred restaurant, a relaxing spa and acres of mature gardens adjoining a prestigious golf club, 5 km (3 miles) north of the city. ⓐ Carrer de la Vinagrella s/n. ❶ 971 787100.

Convent de la Missió €€€ An ultra-modern four-star hotel in a converted monastery near La Rambla, with spartan white interiors, a Zen-inspired rooftop terrace and a whirlpool and sauna in the ancient crypt. ⓐ Carrer de la Missió 7a. ❶ 971 227347; Ⓦ www.conventdelamissio.com

Palau Ca Sa Galesa €€€ Palma's most exclusive hideaway – a sumptuous 17th-century *palacio* at the heart of the medieval city, crammed with antiques and artworks by Calder and Miró. There is a rooftop terrace, a Roman vaulted basement with a small pool, sauna and gym and complimentary tea is served daily in the Monet kitchen. ⓐ Carrer Miramar 8. ❶ 971 715400; Ⓦ www.palaciocasagalesa.com

Puro Oasis Urbano €€€ Palma's funkiest hotel is ideal for a hedonistic getaway weekend. Its 24 white rooms with jellybean-coloured accents smack of Ibizan hippie-chic, and its cool clientele while away the hours in the rooftop hot-tub and in the sophisticated after-hours bar with its resident DJ. ⓐ Carrer Montenegro 12. ❶ 971 425450; Ⓦ www.purohotel.com

🔺 *The Valparaíso Palace is one of Palma's top hotels*

Valparaíso Palace €€€ Set in magnificent gardens a short distance from the city centre, this huge five-star hotel has a luxurious new spa and wellness centre. ⓐ Carrer Francisco Vidal Sureda 23.
ⓣ 971 400300; Ⓦ www.grupotel.com

YOUTH HOSTEL
Albergue Juvenil Platja de Palma € One of just two youth hostels on the island, about 20 minutes out of town, and only open in high season (February to October). With just 65 rooms, it is frequently block-booked by school groups. ⓐ Costa Brava 13. ⓣ 971 260892.
Ⓝ Bus 15 or 23.

THE BEST OF PALMA

Palma is relatively small, compact and easy to explore on foot, with its leafy promenades, its maze of ancient streets, its stepped alleyways and sun-soaked squares flanked by ageing mansions and magnificent palaces. Most of the main city sights lie within the old town and along the seafront. Apart from one or two excursions to the outskirts and neighbouring resorts, there is little need to stray beyond the ancient boundaries of the old town.

Attractions of special appeal to families with children are described on pages 147–150.

TOP 10 ATTRACTIONS

- **La Seu** This mighty sandstone cathedral is undoubtedly the jewel in Palma's crown (see page 58).

- **Palau Reial de l'Almudaina** This ancient palace bears witness to centuries of conflict between the Moors and the Christians (see page 62).

- **The Seafront & Port** Everything from tiny traditional fishing boats to super-yachts, naval vessels and massive cruise liners (see page 83).

- **Es Baluard, Museum d'Art Modern i Contemporani** Palma's newest museum contains a formidable collection of modern art (see page 87).

- **Castell de Bellver** The only circular castle in Spain, with a truly *bell ver* (beautiful view) of Palma Bay from its rooftop. (see page 85).

- **Museu de Mallorca** A quick overview of the island from prehistory to the 20th century (see page 70).

- **Sant Francesc** The tranquil cloisters here provide respite from the crowded alleys of the old town (see page 65).

- **Plaça del Mercat and Plaça Weyler** Admire the *joie de vivre* of the *Modernista* architecture here (see page 69).

- **Fundació Pilar i Joan Miró** The museum and studio of the island's greatest 'adopted' artist (see page 106).

- **Mountain train to Sóller** The vintage train ride through the Mallorcan countryside to Sóller is a journey not to be missed (see page 128).

⬇ *The architecture of the Palau March is as surreal as some of its paintings*

Here's a quick guide to seeing the best of Palma, depending on the time you have available.

HALF-DAY: PALMA IN A HURRY

If you only have a few hours, start at the Parc de la Mar, where the magnificent golden sandstone cathedral, La Seu, is reflected perfectly in the lake. Climb the steps of the medieval walls and visit the interior of the cathedral, then explore the old Arab quarter – a warren of medieval streets where the wealthy Catalan merchants built their palaces during the city's maritime heyday. Pop into the Museu de Mallorca – with a grasp of the island's colourful history, walks around town are all the more rewarding. Grab a coffee in a locals' bar, before returning for a tour of the Almudaina. Then relax in the old royal gardens, S'Hort del Rei, with their shady orange trees, fountains and modern sculptures.

1 DAY: TIME TO SEE A LITTLE MORE

After you have done the recommended half-day sightseeing, add some shopping to your itinerary: stroll along the tree-lined boulevards of Passeig des Born and La Rambla, and explore the craft shops and boutiques in the streets around Plaça Major. Alternatively, take in an art gallery: Es Baluard is a must to see the local impressionist paintings of the island, and it also has a wonderful terrace café overlooking the bay for light refreshment. At the end of the day, enjoy some al fresco tapas in one of the bars of Plaça Llotja, before exploring the maze of tiny lanes and alleyways behind the square, whose myriad restaurants, bars and clubs ensure an excellent evening out.

> ● *You can see virtually the whole of the city from Castel de Bellver*

2–3 DAYS: SHORT CITY-BREAK

The extra days give you plenty of time to explore the waterfront. The best image of Palma is from the sea, so take a boat trip round the bay, or stroll along the Passeig Marítim past fishing boats, yachts and Mediterranean motor cruisers, until you reach the westernmost part of the port with its naval vessels and huge cruise liners. There are some well-placed cafés en route. You may also have enough time to hop on a bus to Castel de Bellver, to the caves at Genova or to Cala Major to see the Fundació Pilar i Joan Miró.

LONGER: ENJOYING PALMA TO THE FULL

A longer stay enables you to soak up the café culture of the old town, to top up your tan on the beaches in the Badia de Palma, and to check out some of the city's vibrant late-night clubs and bars. You should also take at least one trip out of town (see pages 113–140).

Something for nothing

Palma is the perfect destination for budget travellers, as there are plenty of sights and attractions to amuse you, without the need to spend a single euro.

For a taste of ancient Palma, explore the old historic centre – a picturesque maze of narrow streets and stepped alleyways fanning out around the cathedral with hidden fountain-filled squares, ornate churches and beautifully restored mansions. Peer into their elegant courtyards with their flower-bedecked patios and arcaded balconies. Look out also for the amazing statuary and carvings throughout the city, from the celebrated 'Sling Thrower' in S'Hort del Rei (the King's Gardens, see page 62) to the finials of the Ajuntament. For a taste of local colour, join the residents of Palma window-shopping in Avinguda Jaume III and stroll along the seafront for yet more historic sights and fantastic viewpoints.

If all that walking sounds too energetic, soak up the atmosphere in the city squares, or while away the hours watching street performers in Plaça Major and in the leafy boulevards of El Born and La Rambla, where you will find everything from buskers and magicians to human statues. Alternatively, escape the city bustle and people-watch on the floral terraces of the Jardines de Sa Faixina; or take a book, find a shady seat and drift off to sleep to the soothing sound of the gently splashing pools and fountains in the old royal gardens, the Hort del Rei.

Even art aficionados on a tight budget need not be disappointed, as Palma boasts numerous galleries with free entry, including Ses Voltes, Sa Llotja, Fundación La Caixa, Fundación Sa Nostra, Can Balaguer and Can Solleric, as well as a small Sport Museum and a Military Museum. Ask the tourist office for details of their exhibitions.

◆ *The atmosphere of old Palma, in spots such as the Sant Francesc cloisters, costs nothing to enjoy*

If you're lucky, you may even experience one of Palma's 'free' parties, should your visit coincide with one of their big fiestas (see page 9), when city-dwellers take to the streets in fancy dress in enormous parades, with brass bands, floats and fireworks.

When it rains

The *good* news is that it rarely rains in Palma. When it does, don't despair! The city has plenty of attractions to cheer up the dullest, wettest day.

For starters, the city abounds in museums and galleries to suit all tastes and interests. Immerse yourself in history at the Arab Baths, the Museu Diocesà or the Museo de Mallorca. Visit one of numerous art galleries, or seek refuge from the elements in the city's magnificent churches. The Basílica de Sant Francesc is best-known for its beautiful cloisters, while Sant Miquel is among the most popular churches in town. La Seu, the 'Cathedral of Light', is one of the largest and most beautiful Gothic cathedrals in the world and a must-see whatever the weather. An ideal way of travelling from sight to sight is on the open-top hop-on-hop-off Sightseeing Bus (see page 56). Obviously you wouldn't want to sit upstairs if it's raining, but there's always plenty of room on the lower floor, and it is a better mode of transport than catching numerous taxis or walking in the rain.

If the rain persists head to one of the large shopping centres – Porto Pi (see page 109) on the seafront, or Festival Park (see page 104) for factory outlet shopping and family fun just outside town – or to the cinema. Most complexes show original-version movies, subtitled in Castilian Spanish.

Better still, do as the locals and pass the time in the countless cafés and bars. There's always an excuse to nip in for a drink, whether it's coffee and *churros* for breakfast, a quick mid-morning espresso pick-me-up, tapas and *tertulia* (a chat with friends) for lunch or an early-evening get-together with friends for a *copa* (a quick sherry, liqueur or cognac) before dinner. You could even sample several bars in one evening, by following the Andalusian custom of the *tapeo*, moving from bar to bar just sampling one tapas dish in each. *Buen apetito*!

🔊 *Cool and peaceful, and dry when it's raining – the Arab Baths*

On arrival

There is no need to worry about your arrival in Palma. It is a small city which is easy to navigate your way around on foot or by public transport, and the tourist office provides excellent maps to help you. The locals are also usually more than willing to help any visitor.

TIME DIFFERENCES

Like the rest of Spain, Mallorca follows Central European Time (CET), which is one hour ahead of Greenwich Mean Time (GMT+1). When it's 12.00 in Palma, this is the time back home:

Australia Eastern Standard Time 20.00, Central Standard Time 19.30, Western Standard Time 18.00.
New Zealand 22.00.
South Africa 12.00.
UK and Republic of Ireland 11.00.
USA and Canada Newfoundland Time 07.30, Atlantic Canada Time 07.00, Eastern Time 06.00, Central Time 05.00, Mountain Time 04.00, Pacific Time 03.00, Alaska 02.00.

ARRIVING

By air

Son Sant Joan Airport, Palma's only international airport, is located 10 km (6 miles) east of the city centre and is easily accessible from all parts of the island. The high-tech, modern terminal is one of the busiest in Europe during summer months, and has excellent facilities, including 24-hour first-aid services and a post office in the Check-in area (second floor), a pharmacy and a bank in Departures (fourth floor) and several cash dispensers and exchange booths in

⬛ *A spot of sun-worship will help you recover from the rigours of air travel*

the Arrivals (ground floor). Other services include VIP lounges, and a
good selection of shops, bars and restaurants, including a 24-hour bar
and a 24-hour cafeteria. There is no left-luggage facility and the lost
property office is situated in Arrivals on the ground floor. Airport
information desks (❶ 971 225000) can be found in Arrivals, Departures
and at Check-in, and there is a tourist information desk on the ground
floor (❶ 971 789556). Car hire desks are located in Arrivals and include
such companies as Avis, Betacar-Europcar and Hertz.

If you're not hiring a car, a taxi into Palma (from outside Door 4
on the Arrivals level) will take approximately 15 minutes and cost
around €15. Alternatively, bus 1 runs from the airport to Plaça
d'Espanya in Palma city centre approximately every 15 minutes from
06.10 until 01.10. The journey takes around 30 minutes and costs
€1.85. There is a bus stop outside Door 4 of the Arrivals area and
another in front of the multi-storey car park.

By rail

Mallorca's main train station is located at Plaça d'Espanya in Palma. A narrow-gauge railway runs from Palma to Inca, Sa Pobla and Manacor. The journey lasts about 50 minutes. An old wooden train runs to Palma from the mountain town of Sóller, and takes about 55 minutes. The resort of Port de Sóller on the northern coast is a short ride to Sóller by an equally old wooden tram. ☎ 971 752245 (Inca-Manacor) and ☎ 971 752051 (Sóller) for information.

By bus

Mallorca's main bus terminal is located at Plaça d'Espanya in the city centre. An efficient bus network connects all the main towns in Mallorca to Palma. ☎ 971 176970 for information.

Driving

Driving in Mallorca is relatively straightforward and it is easy to access all parts of Palma from the *Via Cintura* (ring road), which is clearly signed from the airport. Remember to drive on the right and stick to the speed limits: 120 km/h on motorways, 100 km/h on main road, 90 km/h on other roads except in urban areas where it is 60 km/h unless otherwise signposted.

If you are planning to drive in Palma, it is worth investing in a detailed street map and familiarising yourself with the main streets in advance. Although main sights are clearly signposted, there are several one-way systems that can be confusing. Parking can also be difficult. Public car parks are expensive and it is virtually impossible to find a vacant place in the streets. Your best bet is to find a parking lot marked in blue with a *Zona Blava* (Blue Zone) sign, and to purchase a ticket (valid for 30–120 minutes depending on the area) from a nearby parking meter. Tickets are generally required on

weekdays 09.00–14.00 and 17.00–20.00, and on Saturdays
09.00–14.00. Failing that, the most popular underground car parks
are by the cathedral and under Plaça Major, so be prepared to
queue.

FINDING YOUR FEET

On first impression, Palma appears to be a bustling Mediterranean
city, but the pace of life here is surprisingly relaxed. The people are
laid-back, friendly and happy to help tourists. It is also a safe city
with a low crime rate. However, it is advisable to take the normal
precautions you would in any city. Don't carry excess cash, and use

---

IF YOU GET LOST, TRY ...

Excuse me, do you speak English?
Perdone, ¿habla usted inglés?
Perdoene, ¿ahbla oosteth eengless?

**Excuse me, is this the right way to the old town/the city
centre/the tourist office/ the station/the bus station?**
Perdone, ¿por aquí se va a el casco antiguo/al centro de la ciudad/
oficina de turísmo/la estación de trenes/estación de autobuses?
*Perdoneh, ¿porr akee seh bah ah el kasko antigwo/al thentroe de
la theeoodath/offeetheena deh toorismoe/la estatheeon de
trenes/estatheeon dey awtoebooses?*

Can you point to it on my map?
¿Puede señalármelo en el mapa?
¿Pwede senyarlarmeloe en el mapa?

Arquitecte Forteza

General Riera

Capita Salom

Bornheim

Via Alemanya

Comte de Salent

31 de Diciembre

Aragon

La Rambla

Av. Jaume III

Sant Jaume

Sant Miquel

Es Baluard

Carrer de l'Unió

Passeig des Born

Railway and Bus Station

Arago

Almudaina

Alomar i Vilalonga

Manacor

eig de Sagrera

La Seu

Parc de la Mar

Avinguda de Gabriel

Joan Maragall

Pas eig 'O'

0   500m   1km

the hotel safe for valuable goods; don't leave anything visible in a parked car; beware of pickpockets in crowded places; don't leave valuables on the beach or poolside, and stick to well-lit, populated areas by night.

ORIENTATION

Palma is compact enough to explore easily on foot. The city divides into two distinct areas: the old town surrounding the cathedral, to the east of the Passeig des Born, and the city centre and main nightlife area, to the west of the Passeig des Born, including the harbour and promenade area, called the Passeig Marítim. The ancient maze of side streets can be confusing, so familiarise yourself with the main avenues in the city centre – Passeig de la Rambla, Carrer de l'Unio, Avinguda Jaume III and Passeig des Born – which interconnect and split the capital neatly into two. Should you get lost, use such unmissable landmarks as the cathedral and the Bay of Palma to help you get your bearings.

The maps in this book show all the main streets and sights, but for further exploring, invest in a detailed street map, obtainable anywhere in Palma.

GETTING AROUND

The bus network is excellent and links the capital to most places on the island. It is also the best way to visit the city suburbs. All buses pass through the main bus station in Plaça d'Espanya, and route maps can be found at every bus stop and at the tourist information office. The driver is paid on entering, so have small change ready, and keep your ticket for inspection during the journey. The Bono-Bus

> *Galeras are a romantic and leisurely way to do some sightseeing*

Arquitecte Forteza

16,19

6

Capità Salom 12,27

General Riera

31 de Dicembre

4,5,6

Via Alemanya

Comte de Sallent

Aragón

La Rambla

Sant Miquel

3

2,3,6,7,50

Passeig des Born — Sant Jaume

5,7,15,50

Railway and
Bus Station

s Baluard

Aragó

2

5

1,50

Almudaina

Alomar y Villalonga

Manacor 7,14,18

La Seu

Parc de la Mar

12

Plg de Sagrera

19,50

Avinguda de
Gabriel

Joan Maragall

Pas. elg. 'O'

0   500m   1km

1,15,17,23,31

Bus route

scheme offers books of 10 bus tickets, available from most tobacconists – a definite saving if you intend to use the bus frequently.

The Palma City Sightseeing Bus is a good way to get your bearings. It leaves every 20 minutes from various stops around the city, starting from the Almudaina (Carrer Conquistador), and you can hop on and off at 16 stops (otherwise the round trip takes about 2 hrs) at the main city sights (Ⓦ www.city-sightseeing.com).

White taxis can be hailed in the street or picked up at ranks, but they are an expensive option. A green roof-light marked *Lliure* or *Libre* indicates they are available for hire. *Galeras* or horse-drawn carriages are an alternative choice for sightseeing in Palma. There are ranks beside the cathedral and the Passeig de Sagrera, with a list of fares. Or hire a bicycle from Ciclos Bimont (Ⓐ Plaça Progrés 19. ☎ 971 731866) and enjoy the 4.5 km (3 mile) cycle lane along the seafront.

CAR HIRE

It is only worthwhile hiring a car if you are heading out of town to explore the island. There are several hire car companies at the airport, although pre-booking via your airline's affiliates should secure you reduced rates.

Avis Ⓐ Passeig Marítim 16. ☎ 971 286233. Ⓐ Aeropuerto.
☎ 971 789187.
Hertz Ⓐ Passeig Marítim 13. ☎ 971 734737. Ⓐ Aeropuerto.
☎ 971 789670.
Betacar-Europcar Ⓐ Passeig Marítim 19. ☎ 971 737589. Ⓐ Aeropuerto.
☎ 971 789135.

Ⓞ *Old Palma is overlooked by the fortress of San Parc, which now houses the city's newest museum, Es Baluard*

THE CITY OF
Palma

East of Passeig des Born

To the east of the city's main thoroughfare, the Passeig des Born, lies the historic centre of Palma. Here you will find the very essence of Mallorca's capital city – the magnificent cathedral overlooking a harbour of mega-yachts; cobbled streets leading to hidden sun-drenched squares flanked by ancient palaces and exuberant churches; avant-garde art galleries; leafy promenades; *Modernista* architecture, superb shopping, and an excellent choice of pavement cafés, restaurants and tapas bars. What's more, the district is small and compact, and easy to explore on foot.

SIGHTS & ATTRACTIONS

La Seu (Cathedral)

Palma's marvellous Gothic cathedral occupies a prominent position overlooking the harbour at the edge of the old city. For centuries it has been the symbol of Palma and a welcome sight to home-bound sailors, standing proudly out on the city's skyline.

It is said that when Jaume I set sail to conquer Mallorca from the Moors in 1229, he vowed to build a cathedral large enough to reach the sky if his mission succeeded. The result was this remarkable 'Cathedral of Light', one of the largest and most beautiful Gothic cathedrals in the world, and an expression of his political power – strategically built on the seafront for all to see, on the site of the former Great Mosque.

The foundation stone for the cathedral was laid by Jaume in 1230, but it has been extensively remodelled over the years and was not completed until 1601. As a consequence the exterior, built from local golden Santanyí sandstone, demonstrates a variety of

Comte de Sallent

Via Alemanya

Via Portugal

Passeig de Mallorca

C Bisbe Campins

Passeig d' Oliver

Av Juan March

Sant Miquel

Plaça d' Espanya

Passeig de la Rambla

Plaça Olivar

Sant Jaume

Jaume III

L Unió

La Caixa

Museu d' Art Espanyol Contemporari

Plaça Weyler

Plaça del Mercat

Plaça Major

Passeig des Born

Plaça Cort

ℹ️

Plaça Santa Eulalia

Ajuntament

Conquistador

Palau March Museu

Av. Antoni Maura

S'Hort del Rei

Almudaina

La Seu (cathedral)

Passeig Uruguay

Basílica de Sant Francesc

Museu de Mallorca

Museu Diocesá

Banys Arabs

Parc de la Mar

Pas eig Sagrera

N

0   250m   500m

architectural styles, although Gothic predominates, with its massive flying buttresses, turrets and pinnacles.

The interior is most striking for its sheer proportions. The central nave alone is 121 m (400ft) long and is supported by 20 m (66ft) high pencil-thin pillars. The stained-glass windows are impressive too, especially the huge 15th-century one above the presbytery. Much of the interior was modified at the start of the 20th century by the famous Catalan architect Antoni Gaudí (see page 12), who worked here over a period of years, adding electric lighting and constructing the enormous canopy which hangs over the High Altar, symbolising the Crown of Thorns. The cathedral is entered through the northern door, where alms were dispensed to the poor.

ⓐ Plaça Almoina, s/n. ❶ 971 723130. ◗ June–Sept: 10.00–18.15 Mon–Fri, 10.00–14.15 Sat; Nov–Mar: 10.00–15.15 Mon–Fri, 10.00–14.15 Sat; Apr–May and Oct 10.00–16.15, Sat 10.00–14.15. Closed Sun (except during High Mass). Admission charge.

Parc de la Mar

The mighty city walls, the cathedral and the Palau Reial de l'Almudaina provide a striking backdrop for this large seafront park, built in the 1960s on land reclaimed from the sea. With its palm-shaded terraces, superb children's playground and outdoor cafés, it is one of the capital's most popular outdoor spaces to relax in year round. What's more, it also provides the most photogenic views of the cathedral, perfectly reflected in its ornamental lake.

◗ *Palma's La Seu must be one of the best-sited cathedrals in the world*

Palau Reial de l'Almudaina

Palma's magnificent Royal Palace seems to rise out of the city walls on the seafront beside the cathedral. There has been a palace here since the Muslim governors built their *alcázar* or fortress soon after the Arab conquest. Although it was later converted into Gothic style, some elements of Islamic architecture remain, including the loggia and the Arc de la Drassana Reial, the entrance to the royal shipyards that once stood alongside the palace. The *almudaina* (meaning 'citadel') later became the residence of the kings of Mallorca, and it is still the official residence of the Spanish royal family today. Visits are by guided tour only, starting in the central courtyard, and take in the Chapel of Santa Ana, the palace museum and the state apartments.

🅐 Carrer Palau Reial. ☏ 971 214134. 🕓 Oct–Mar 10.00–13.15, 16.00–17.15 Mon–Fri, 10.00–13.15 Sat; Apr–Sept 10.00–17.45 Mon–Fri, 10.00–13.15 Sat. Admission charge.

THE SLING THROWER

The Balearic archipelago is thought to have taken its name from the Greek word *ballein* meaning 'to sling', and a statue in S'Hort del Rei commemorates Mallorca's famous *honderos* (slingers) who defended the island from attack.

S'Hort del Rei (The King's Garden)

Escape from the hustle and bustle of the city and enjoy an afternoon siesta amid the flowers, fountains and statuary in this cool, fragrant garden at the foot of the Palau de l'Almudaina. Look out for the celebrated *honderos* statue (see feature box above) and

also Joan Miró's *Egg*. This sculpture marks the start of the Tourist
Office's walking tours of the city (see page 20) and also the hop-on-
hop-off open-top bus tours (see page 56).

ⓐ Avinguda Antonio Maura.

⬤ *The magnificent Palau Reial de l'Almudaina*

Banys Arabs (Arab Baths)

The ornate columns and elegant domes of these baths, dating from the 10th century, are one of the few surviving monuments from Mallorca's long period of Moorish rule. From 902 until 1229 there was a Moorish city, the Medina Mayurqa, here. The baths were originally part of a palace belonging to an Arab nobleman. Built in Roman style, they were used as health spas and meeting places. Bathers would move between the hot, steamy *caldarium* and the cooler *tepidarium*, before cooling off in the courtyard. Today the fountain-splashed garden is still a delightful place to relax, with its cacti, palms and citrus trees.

ⓐ Carrer Serra 7. ⓣ 971 721549. ⓛ Apr–Nov 09.00–19.30; Dec–Mar 09.00–18.00. Admission charge.

Ajuntament

Palma's imposing 17th-century town hall is not actually open to the public, but should you pass it when the grand main doors are open, peek inside and you will catch a glimpse of the *gigantones*, folkloric 'giants' that parade the streets whenever Palma has a fiesta. Join locals relaxing on the stone benches surrounding this impressive building, and be sure to gaze skywards to see the unusual wood carvings overhanging the facade. They are the work of a naval carpenter, which is why they look more like the figureheads of ships than traditional finials.

ⓐ Plaça Cort. ⓣ 971 225900. ⓦ www.a-palma.es

Basilica de Sant Francesc (Basilica of St Francis)

Visit this impressive Gothic church and you will be greeted outside

◐ *Make for the cloisters of Saint Francesc for some peace and quiet*

by a statue of Friar Junípero Serra, the Mallorcan Franciscan friar who, during a pilgrimage to America, founded California. The sober facade belies a surprisingly ornate interior, with lavish side chapels and an exuberant high altarpiece. But the *pièce de resistance* here is undoubtedly the adjoining 14th-century cloister, with its central fountain dating from 1638 and pointed archways, which give the cloister an almost Moorish feel. Shaded by lemon trees, the cloister has been declared a national monument and is a veritable oasis of peace.

ⓐ Plaça Sant Francesc 7. ☎ 971 712695. ⏰ 09.30–12.30, 15.30–18.00 Mon–Sat, 09.30–12.00 Sun. Donation requested.

Plaça Major

This beautiful arcaded square at the heart of a busy shopping district is especially popular for its pavement cafés, street entertainment and artisans' stalls and makes an ideal place to pause during a shopping spree. Don't overlook the buildings, though! This attractive square was built in the early 1800s, surrounded by four-storey apricot-coloured buildings with green shutters, and with an arched portico on the ground floor containing a wide variety of shops. The city's main fish and vegetable market was here until the 1950s, when it was relocated to its larger site (Mercat Olivar) nearby. Beneath the square is a shopping centre and an underground car park, where remains of a fortified Moorish wall were discovered during excavation work. But it's the local shopping that is the main crowd puller here; narrow, labyrinthine streets lead off in all directions from the square, each one packed with boutiques and craft shops.

● *Plaça Major is an oasis of relaxation in the busiest part of Palma*

Plaça del Mercat & Plaça Weyler

These bustling squares contain some of the capital's most dazzling architecture. Plaça Weyler boasts Palma's first *Modernista* building – the ornamental Gran Hotel, constructed by the Catalan architect Lluis Domènech i Montaner in 1902, which has been magnificently restored and today contains the Fundació La Caixa (see page 72). Opposite, the Forn des Teatre bakery is probably the city's most photographed shop, with its attractive green and yellow *Modernista* decor. The adjoining leafy square of Plaça del Mercat contains two further *Modernista* buildings – Pensió Menorquina and Can Casasayas, commissioned in 1908 by wealthy Palma resident Josep Casasayas, their rippling facades decorated with butterfly and fern motifs. The square also contains a statue of the island's most famous politician, Antoni Maura (several times prime minister of Spain at the start of the 20th century), and the Palau de Justicia, Palma's courthouse.

La Rambla

La Rambla has been one of the city's main promenades for many years. Once the main watercourse through the city, today this impressive tree-lined avenue is filled with the colourful stalls of Palma's daily flower market.

CULTURE

Palma prides itself on being a city of art and culture and many of its major museums and galleries can be found in the old town. But don't just look at the contents of the collections, as many of the

One of Palma's most photographed sights is in the Plaça del Mercat

69

buildings warrant attention, too. Some of the museums are housed in beautifully restored Renaissance *palacios*, and one gallery is contained within the former Gran Hotel, one of the city's finest *Modernista* buildings with its impressive, recently restored facade.

Museu de Mallorca

Appropriately enough, Mallorca's leading history museum is contained within a magnificent 17th-century palace, built on the foundations of one of the island's earliest Arab houses, and located in an atmospheric part of the old town. The interior provides a complete overview of Mallorcan history, with its huge range of artefacts, from Talaiotic and Roman tools and jewellery to Moorish mementos, early Christian art and religious paintings. Temporary exhibitions on local topics add to the museum's appeal.

ⓐ Carrer Portella 5. ⓕ 971 717540. ⓛ 10.00–18.30 Tues–Sat, 10.30–13.30 Sun. Admission charge.

Museu Diocesà

This quirky museum, located just behind the cathedral in the Episcopal Palace, is packed with religious artefacts, historic treasures and holy relics from around the island, as well as an impressive collection of ceramics. Highlights include Moorish tapestries, Jaume II's jasper sepulchre and a portrait of St George slaying the dragon with medieval Palma in the background.

ⓐ Carrer Calders 2. ⓕ 971 213100. ⓛ 10.00–13.00, 16.00–19.00 Wed. Admission charge.

Palau March Museu (March Palace Museum)

A beautiful palace in the city centre, containing a variety of treasures including murals by the great painter Josep Maria Sert,

and some fascinating 16th- and 17th-century maps of
Mediterranean Europe. The courtyard contains an impressive
collection of contemporary sculptures, with works by Rodin, Dalí and
Moore.

ⓐ Palau Reial 18. ⓣ 971 711122. ⓦ www.fundbmarch.es ⓛ Apr–Oct
10.00–18.30 Mon–Fri, 10.00–14.00 Sat; Nov–Mar 10.00–17.00
Mon–Fri, 10.00–14.00 Sat.

Museu d'Art Espanyol Contemporani – Fundación Juan March

A small but dazzling display of 20th-century Spanish art, collected
by Mallorcan banker Juan March, including some priceless treasures
by Picasso, Miró and Salvador Dalí, as well as the Mallorcan-born
Miquel Barceló.

ⓐ Carrer de Sant Miquel 11. ⓣ 971 713515. ⓛ 10.00–18.30 Mon–Fri,
10.30–14.00 Sat. Admission free.

🔺 *Palau March - quirky art in a beautiful palace*

Fundació La Caixa

This art gallery in the former Gran Hotel, Palma's first quality hotel (see page 70), has a permanent exhibition of Mallorcan paintings as well as changing temporary displays, and a popular art bookshop. The ground-floor café-bar is one of Palma's smartest meeting places, and the building itself, a fine example of Catalan Modernista architecture, is also worth a look.

ⓐ Plaça Weyler 3. ❶ 971 720111. ◗ 10.00–21.00 Tues–Sat, 10.00–14.00 Sun. Admission free.

Ca'n Rei

The intricate coloured facade of mosaics and its ornate wrought-ironwork make this house the finest *Modernista* building in Mallorca. Built by a local silversmith, Lluis Forteza Rey, it shows strong influences of Gaudí (see page 12). ⓐ Carrer Bolseria.

RETAIL THERAPY

Start your shopping spree in the pedestrianised streets leading off Plaça Major – where there are plenty of small, reasonably priced specialist shops, interspersed with shoe shops, fashion designers and jewellery boutiques – or explore the trendy boutiques lining Carrer Sant Nicolas and the other narrow streets behind Passeig des Born and Carrer de l'Unio. Also, the best markets are in this part of town: flowers at La Rambla and picnic supplies at Mercat Olivar.

Specialist shops

Artesanies Pol The brightly coloured Mallorcan ceramics here make ideal gifts. ⓐ Carrer de l'Unió 13. ❶ 971 724299.

Casa Bonet A truly Mallorcan shop serving old-fashioned, traditionally made *bordados* (embroidered goods). ⓐ Plaça Frederic Chopin 2. ⓣ 971 722117.

Casa del Olivo Everything in this tiny workshop is handmade from olive-wood. ⓐ Carrer Pescateria Vella 4.

Fiol Palma's best second-hand bookshop, with an excellent stock of books in English and various other languages. ⓐ Carrer Oms 45a. ⓣ 971 721428.

Imaginarium A magical toy shop, full of sturdy educational toys, games and witty children's furnishings. ⓐ Plaça Weyler 11. ⓣ 971 714340. ⓦ www.imaginarium.es ⓒ 10.00–21.00 Mon–Sat.

Vidrierías Gordiola The best shop in town for glassware. ⓐ Carrer de la Victoria 2. ⓣ 971 711541.

Fashion
Adolfo Domínguez One of Spain's most famous designers, Domínguez is famed for introducing linen suits in the 1980s with the slogan 'wrinkles are fashionable'. ⓐ Carrer Colom 9. ⓣ 971 721565. ⓦ www.adolfo-dominguez.com

Blanc Bleu Stylish, sporty fashions for both sexes. ⓐ Carrer Sant Nicolau 22. ⓣ 971 716983.

Eurocarnavales For a bit of fun, check out this eccentric store, which sells costumes for fiestas. ⓐ Carrer de Porta de Jesus 16. ⓣ 971 722627.

Mango This popular Spanish chainstore brims with cheap, trendy designs for the truly fashionable. ⓐ Avinguda Jaume III 9. ⓣ 971 713896. ⓦ www.mango.com

S'Avarca de Menorca Traditional Menorcan leather sandals for men, women and children. ⓐ Carrer Sant Domingo 14. ⓣ 971 712058. ⓦ www.savarca.com

Yanko This smart boutique sells exclusively Yanko shoes – a Mallorcan brand of beautifully designed shoes at moderate prices. ⓐ Carrer Sant Nicolau 12. ⓣ 971 714071.

Gastronomic
Breweriana If beer's your tipple, this is the shop for you, with over 200 different varieties of bottled beers and glasses. ⓐ Carrer de Sant Jaume 20. ⓣ 971 229406.

Can Frasquet Palma's top chocolate shop. An absolute must for chocoholics. ⓐ Carrer Orfila 4. ⓣ 971 721354.

Colmado St Domingo This tiny grocery store is probably Palma's most photogenic shop, and it sells all kinds of tasty local foods such as *sobrasada*, fig bread, olives and nuts. ⓐ Carrer Sant Domingo 5.

Forn Fondo Shop here for fresh *ensaimadas* (see page 26). ⓐ Carrer de l'Unió. ⓣ 971 711634.

Mercat Olivar Palma's main market is located in a large hall near

---

❶ *It seems a shame to disturb the perfect arrangement by buying something*

🔺 *Montana - definitely the place for sausages*

Plaça d'Espanya, with fresh produce on the ground floor and meat and cheese upstairs. There are also several cheap tapas stands. 🅐 Plaça Olivar. 🕐 971 724650.

La Montana This tiny shop with hundreds of sausages hanging from the ceiling is one of the city's top delicatessens. 🅐 Carrer de Jaume II 29.

TAKING A BREAK

Whether it's coffee or ice cream, a refreshing drink or a light lunch, you'll find a large and varied selection of eateries in and around the old town. Some are hidden down cool, shady streets in the old Arab quarter, others are clustered around busy squares, and are great for people-watching. You could even grab a snack from the market stalls at Mercat Olivar (see page 74). Some of the bars and restaurants in the 'After Dark' section (see page 78) also serve food and drinks during the day.

Bar Bosch This café-bar at the top of the Passeig des Born has long been one of the city's most popular meeting places for a coffee and a light snack. ⓐ Plaça Rei Joan Carles I. ⓣ 971 721131. ⓛ 08.00–03.00 Mon–Sat.

Café Cappuccino The perfect place to people-watch, or simply to relax on the shaded terrace with a coffee and a cake. ⓐ Carrer Conquistador 13. ⓣ 971 717272.

Ca'n Joan de S'Aigo Pastries, cakes, almond ice cream and scrumptious hot chocolate are all on the menu at this 200-year-old café in a narrow winding street. ⓐ Carrer Ca'n Sanc 10. ⓣ 971 725760. ⓛ 08.00–21.15 Wed–Mon.

Diplomatic There are no airs or graces at this locals' restaurant. Just good, honest home cooking, excellent lunch menus and the capital's tastiest *arròz negre* (savoury rice blackened wth squid ink). ⓐ Carrer Palau Reial 5. ⓣ 971 726482.

Fundació La Caixa An elegant bar in Palma's first *Modernista* building (see page 72), serving excellent salads, sandwiches and bar snacks. ⓐ Plaça Weyler 3. ⓣ 971 716858. ⓛ 10.00–21.00 Tues–Sat, 10.00–14.00 Sun.

Tast A modern, informal café-bar, with an open kitchen and an excellent choice of tapas and canapés displayed along a long marble bar. ⓐ Carrer de l'Unio 28. ⓣ 971 729878.

AFTER DARK

This is not Palma's main party district. Nonetheless, there are still some excellent restaurants here to suit all tastes and budgets, and a handful of friendly bars too.

Restaurants

La Bodeguilla € Tradition meets modernity in this intimate tapas bar, which serves over 200 different varieties of wine. Join Palma's smart set and try the *menu degustación* (tasting menu).
ⓐ Carrer Sant Jaume 3. ① 971 718274. ⓦ www.la-bodeguilla.com
🕐 13.00–23.30 Mon–Sat.

La Taberna del Caracol € In one of the oldest buildings in the Old Quarter, serving outstanding tapas with an enormous variety. Sample one or two dishes or try the house speciality, which includes a little of everything.
ⓐ Carrer San Alonso 2. ① 971 714908. 🕐 13.00–15.30, 19.00–24.00 Tues–Sun.

Es Parlament €€ This old-fashioned establishment, in the Balearic Parliament buildings, is known for its squid and its paella *ciega* ('blind paella' – in other words, without bones), and is especially popular among politicians and business people.
① Carrer de Conquistador 11. ① 971 726026.

Refectori €€ Adventurous Mallorquin cuisine in a calm, minimalist setting inside a converted 17th-century convent. Part of hotel Convent de la Missió (see page 36). ⓐ Carrer de la Missió 7a.
① 971 227347.

Sa Premsa €€ A typical Mallorcan cellar-restaurant, with wine vats around the walls, old bullfighting posters on the walls and cheerful service. The food is rustic and hearty, with the emphasis on dishes such as *frito mallorquín* and pork wrapped in cabbage leaves.
ⓐ Plaça Bisbe Berenguer de Palou 8.
ⓣ 971 723529. ⓛ 12.30–16.00, 19.30–23.30 Mon–Sat.

Chopin €€€ Fine Mediterranean cuisine in an intimate, sophisticated setting, with an attractive courtyard garden for romantic al fresco dining. ⓐ Plaza Chopin. ⓣ 971 723556.
ⓛ Closed Sat lunch and all day Sun.

Nightlife

Blond Café A cool café with wireless internet, this is a popular haunt for a late-night drink or simply to chill out on the comfortable sofas and giant cushions of the hip basement lounge.
ⓐ Plaça Salvador Coll 10.
ⓣ 971 213646. ⓦ www.blondcafé.com
ⓛ 09.00–23.00 Mon–Sat (some nights until 03.00).

Teatre Principal One of Palma's top theatre venues, staging predominantly classical drama, comedies and classical music. From March until May it also hosts a light opera season.
ⓐ Carrer de la Riera 2. ⓣ 971 713346 (box office).

Ses Voltes This lively open-air venue occupies the filled-in moat between the inner and outer city walls in the Parc de la Mar and hosts live pop, jazz and rock bands most weekends.
ⓐ Parc de la Mar.

West of Passeig des Born

This large area focuses on Palma's magnificent seafront – the Passeig Marítim – which by day is filled with yachtsmen, fishermen, strolling locals and rollerbladers, and after dusk becomes *the* place to be, with its top-notch restaurants, its lively bars and cool clubs. The greatest density of bars and restaurants is in the narrow alleys behind La Llotja, but the far end of the Passeig Marítim, around the little harbour of Can Barbará, has its fair share of the action too.

But this side of town is not just for the party crowd. It also has its fair share of sights and attractions, including the dazzling new contemporary art gallery, Es Baluard, and the historic Castell de Bellver – one of Palma's greatest landmarks.

SIGHTS & ATTRACTIONS

Passeig des Born

The Passeig des Born has been Palma's main promenade since the early 15th century, when an inlet that once ran here was filled in after a flood, after which it became a popular venue for fiestas, tournaments and jousting matches. In Franco's day the avenue was renamed Paseo de Generalísimo Franco, but the Mallorquíns refused to use the new name, insisting it was still 'El Born'. Today, this grand boulevard is lined with ancient lime trees and flanked by some of the city's smartest shops. Despite the heavy traffic, its central walkway with its flower-filled urns still retains the elegance of bygone days, and its shaded stone benches are a perfect place to rest awhile and watch the world go by.

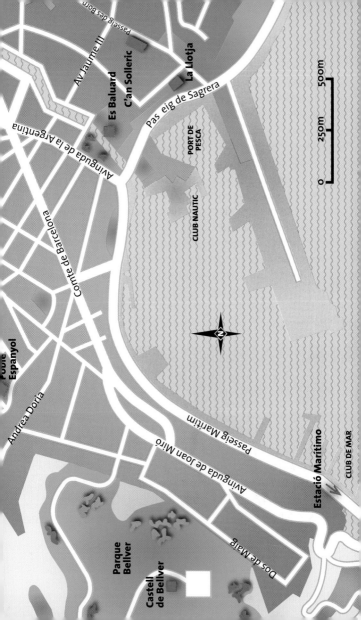

Passeig des Born

Av Jaume III

Es Baluard

C'an Solleric

La Llotja

Avinguda de la Argentina

Pas eig de Sagrera

PORT DE PESCA

CLUB NAUTIC

Comte de Barcelona

Poble Espanyol

Andrea Doria

Avinguda de Joan Miro

Passeig Marítim

Estació Marítimo

CLUB DE MAR

Parque Bellver

Castell de Bellver

Dos de Maig

0   250m   500m

La Llotja

This striking building on the seafront was once the maritime exchange, where shipping merchants and commercial traders would do business. Built between 1426 and 1456 by Mallorca's celebrated architect Guillem Sagrera, it has since been used as a granary, and today it is one of the city's most prominent exhibition halls for cultural exhibitions. The exterior is particularly striking – half castle, half church, with turrets and an angel over the doorway – and stands as testament to Palma's former prosperity as a leading maritime centre. Even if you are not interested in the temporary exhibition that is currently on view, it's worth looking inside just to see the carved pillars and the remarkable rib vaulting in the roof. The area around La Llotja is known for its tapas bars and is particularly lively at night.

➌ Plaça Llotja. ❶ 971 711705. ❷ 11.00–13.45, 17.00–20.45 Tues–Sat, 11.00–13.45 Sun. Closed Mon. Admission free.

🔺 La Llotja - once the commercial hub of Palma

The Seafront & Port

Palma's magnificent seafront has welcomed visitors to its shores for centuries. The seafront promenade, Passeig Marítim, was built in the 1950s to link the old port of Palma, Porto Pi, with the city centre, and it makes a wonderful walk from La Llotja to the passenger ship terminal at the west end of the harbour. Allow about 1¹/2 hours and then you can catch bus 1 or 50 (from Estació Marítimo 2) back to the city centre.

Start on the pedestrian Passeig Sagrera, with its tall palms and historic maritime buildings, including La Llotja and the Renaissance galleried Sea Tribunal (Consulat del Mar), impressively decorated with flags and cannons. Cross over to the sea side, and you will pass the small traditional fishing port (Port de Pesca) and the seemingly endless rows of luxury yachts and motorboats flying the flags of many nations. Even though the fishing port is not as active as in the past, you can still see fishermen sitting on the dock mending their nets. It is a particularly magical experience to stroll here at dusk, when the boat lights are sparkling and the cathedral is illuminated. Continuing along the seafront, look out for the Royal Yacht Club (Reial Club Nautic), patronised by the Spanish royal family and the venue of several annual international sailing regattas. To your right you will see five ruined windmills and, in the distance, an excellent view of the Castell de Bellver gracing the skyline. Further on, there is a small monument commemorating the island's celebrated 15th-century cartographers.

Continue past the massive yachts and ostentatious motor cruisers of the Club de Mar until you reach the ship terminal (Estació Marítimo) at the far end, where naval ships, cruise liners and ferries from mainland Spain dock – and you will soon appreciate Palma's long-standing love affair with the sea. There are also plenty

of bars, cafés and restaurants for refreshments as you go.
If, however, you prefer to explore Palma's glorious bay by boat,
excursion boats offer daytime tours of the harbour from near La
Llotja (🕐 11.00, 12.00, 13.00, 14.00, 15.00, 16.00 Mon–Sat, 11.00, 12.00,
13.00 Sun) and also a night cruise, from opposite the Auditorium
(🕐 June–Sept 22.00 Wed and Sun only). There are also day trips to
Magaluf, Marineland, Cala Vella, Portals Vells, Sant Elm and Camp de
Mar to the west, and to the resorts of Can Pastilla and S'Arenal east
of the city. Contact the tourist office for further details.

Castell de Bellver

This well-preserved circular hill fortress stands sentry above the
port, high in the woods about 3 km (2 miles) from the city centre. It
was built in the 14th century soon after the Catalan conquest, and is
well worth a visit, if only to admire the *bell ver* (beautiful view) of
the capital and the bay from its rooftop balcony.

The castle itself – the only circular one in Spain – was built in
1300 as a royal residence during the reign of King Jaume II and is
especially unusual in its design. The two-storey structure is built
around a central circular courtyard, with three adjoining semi-
circular buttressed towers, and a fourth taller one flanking the
castle. The main floor features rounded arches, while the second
floor has the pointed arches and ribbed vaulting so typical of Gothic
architecture. Over the years the castle has been used as a military
prison and as a mint. Today it houses the Palma History Museum
and the top floor houses a striking collection of classical sculptures.
If you're feeling energetic after your visit, make your way back to the
city centre on foot. The shaded path starts opposite the entrance to

◀ *Pleasure craft jostle in Palma's busy port*

● *The circular layout makes Bellver unique among Spain's castles*

the castle and leads down to Carrer de Bellver and Avinguda de Joan Miró about 1 km below.

● Carrer Camilo José Cela 17, Parc Bellver. ● 971 730658. ● Oct–Mar 08.00–19.15 Mon–Sat, 10.00–17.00 Sun; Apr–Sept 08.00–20.15 Mon–Sat, 10.00–19.00 Sun. ● Bus 50.

CULTURE

Palma's arts scene is booming, and nowhere is this more apparent than at Es Baluard, the latest addition to an impressive list of modern art museums. On a smaller scale, Ca'n Solleric is just one of several cultural centres which have opened in recent years, containing temporary art exhibitions, cafés and bookshops in restored historic buildings.

Es Baluard, Museu d'Art Modern i Contemporani

The capital's newest museum – Es Baluard – is a sensational modern and contemporary art museum, built inside the ancient fortress of Sant Pere and Renaissance walls of Palma, with breath-taking views over the city and the bay. The museum opened in 2004, with four floors of late 19th- to 21st-century art installations. Two floors are devoted to temporary exhibitions. The ground floor and first floor contain the museum's permanent displays, with emphasis on artworks from the Balearics by both local and foreign artists.

The ground floor contains some fantastic impressionist and realist paintings of Palma and Mallorcan landscapes. Local and Catalan artists such as Rossello, Ramus, Mir, Rusinyol, Tàpies and Barceló hang alongside works by Cézanne, Matisse, Dalí, Gauguin and Magritte. One section is dedicated to Miró and includes his 'Mallorca Series' – nine etchings produced in Palma.

Upstairs, the galleries appear to hang in cleverly suspended spaces above the ground. The highlights here include a room devoted entirely to Picasso ceramics, and the rooftop boardwalk – the Passeig de Ronda – which, punctuated with sculptures, has sweeping views of the city and beyond.

Outside the gallery (at ground level), you can walk on the terraces of the old city walls. These, too, have been converted into a brilliant open-air museum, through the imaginative use of brick, glass, aluminium, paving and concrete. The minimalist terrace café is open for lunch and dinner Tuesday to Sunday.

ⓐ Plaça Porta Santa Catalina. ☎ 971 908200. ⓦ www.esbaluard.org
🕐 Oct–mid-June 10.00–20.00 Tues–Sun, mid-June–Sept 10.00–23.00
Tues–Sun. Admission charge.

Ca'n Solleric

This magnificent Italianate building on the city's main promenade,
the Passeig des Born, was constructed for a wealthy family of olive-
oil merchants in 1763. It was converted in 1995 into a modern art
gallery, which hosts a series of temporary exhibitions throughout
the year. Ask at the tourist office for details of what's showing
currently. There is also a small, trendy café-bar adjoining the gallery
which makes an ideal light lunch stop for shoppers, and it is also a
popular meeting place for early-evening drinks.

ⓐ Passeig des Born 27. ☎ 971 722092. 🕐 10.00–13.00, 17.00–21.00
Tues–Sat, 10.00–13.30 Sun, bar closed Sun evening and all day Mon.

Poble Espanyol

This purpose-built 'Spanish Village' at the heart of a residential
district is something of an eccentric attraction. Inside its high walls,
you will find faithful reproductions of around twenty important
Spanish buildings, including El Greco's house in Toledo and
Granada's Alhambra palace. These are then surrounded by typical
houses from various Spanish regions, providing visitors with a
whistle-stop tour of Spanish architecture. In the buildings are
various craft studios that demonstrate a variety of local skills, a café
and a host of souvenir shops selling everything from Mallorcan
pearls to castanets.

▶ *Es Baluard – modern art in an ancient setting*

Carrer Poble Espanyol 39. ☎ 971 737075. 🕐 Apr–Sept 09.00–19.00, Oct–Mar 09.00–18.00 (shops closed on Sat afternoon and Sun). Admission charge.

RETAIL THERAPY

This is the district for serious shoppers, as it embraces Avinguda Jaume III, an elegant arcaded avenue containing Palma's most sophisticated shops, with price tags to match. Here too is the high-quality department store El Corte Inglés, and in Passeig des Born and the surrounding streets you will find an excellent variety of popular chain stores, chic boutiques and specialist shops.

El Corte Inglés One of two branches of Spain's leading department stores in Palma, selling everything from designer fashions to electronics, books, toys, jewellery and cosmetics. There is also a full supermarket, cafeteria and restaurant, and the Gourmet Club delicatessen on the second floor offers over 1000 varieties of wine, oils, cheeses and other gastronomic delights, including ready-made picnic packs for days out. The underground car park is extremely popular for city-centre shoppers. 📍 Avinguda Jaume III 15.
☎ 971 770177. 🌐 www.elcorteingles.es

Mango A nationwide chain of trendy fashion stores, popular with young fashionistas on a budget. 📍 Avinguda Jaume III. ☎ 971
🌐 www.mango.es

⏵ *Take a walk around Poble Espanyol and you won't need to visit the rest of Spain*

El Centro del Vino y del Cava Probably the best selection of wines and cavas in town. ❷ Carrer Bartomeu Rossello-Porcel 19. ☎ 971 452990.

Es Baluard The museum shop of Palma's newest modern art gallery sells an impressive range of arty gifts, calendars, ceramics, mobiles, silk scarves and beautiful coffee-table books on Mallorca. ❷ Plaça Porta Santa Catalina. ☎ 971 908200. ⓦ www.esbaluard.org ⓛ Oct–mid-June 10.00–20.00 Tues–Sun, mid-June–Sept 10.00–23.00 Tues–Sun.

Loewe One of the most celebrated leather-goods companies in the world – for luxury handbags, jackets, shoes and other accessories – in Palma's main shopping street. ❷ Avinguda Jaume III 1. ☎ 971 715275. ⓦ www.loewe.es

Majorica The main city branch of Mallorca's leading cultured pearl manufacturer. ❷ Avinguda Jaume III 11. ☎ 971 725268.

Persépolis With its valuable canvases, period furniture, silver and ceramics, Palma's premier antiques shop is a fascinating place to browse or window-shop. ❷ Avinguda Jaume III. ☎ 971 724539.

Relojería Alemana This upmarket jewellers sells all the top names in designer watches and jewellery (including Tiffany, Bulgari and Cartier), as well as fine silver tableware and Mallorcan grandfather clocks. ❷ Avinguda Jaume III 26. ☎ 971 716712.

TAKING A BREAK

You'll be spoilt for choice of eateries in the La Llotja district of town, with its countless restaurants and tapas bars in the maze of narrow streets and alleys just off Passeig des Born and Avinguda Antoni Maura. Or try the new Es Baluard café-restaurant, which boasts the best terrace views in Palma – perfect for a long lazy lunch.

Bon Lloc One of Palma's few vegetarian restaurants, with a good value four-course set lunch. ⓐ Carrer Sant Feliu 7. ⓣ 971 718617. ⓛ 13.00–16.00 Tues–Sat.

La Boveda This is definitely the best and most popular tapas bar in Palma. Choose from *pa amb oli* (see page 26), cured ham, mussels and octopus, which you eat while standing up against an old wine barrel. ⓐ Carrer Boteria 3. ⓣ 971 714863. ⓛ 13.30–16.00 and 20.30–00.30 Mon–Sat.

Museu Es Baluard Modern Mallorquin al fresco dining on a shaded terrace in Palma or in the cool, white minimalist dining room overlooking the port, with excellent salads, soups and seafood, attached to the city's newest modern art museum. ⓐ Plaça Porta Santa Catalina s/n. ⓣ 971 908199. ⓛ 13.00–16.00, 20.00–23.00 Tues–Sun.

Port Pesquer This chic waterfront café serves delicious fresh fish and tapas from midday to midnight, and has wonderful harbour views from the boardwalk terrace. There's even live music on Thursday and Friday nights. ⓐ Passeig Marítim (near the fishing harbour). ⓣ 971 715220. ⓛ 10.00–02.00 (until 03.00 Thur–Sat).

Xim's Bodeguita One of several hugely popular pavement cafés serving tapas in Plaça Llotja. ⓐ Place Llotja.

AFTER DARK

If you're looking for the trendiest hangouts, this is the district for you. La Llotja boasts the highest density of restaurants and bars, but for night owls the Passeig Marítim is the place to be, with its countless late-bars and nightclubs all revelling to the sounds of the Balearic beat. Also check out the cool, laid-back bars around the small inlet of Can Barbará – this is the latest hotspot in town.

Restaurants

Can Carlos € Tucked down a back-street just off the fashionable Avinguda Jaume III, this traditional-style restaurant specialises in authentic *cuina mallorquina*. Try their tasty *tumbet* or the hearty *frit mallorquí* (see page 24). ⊘ Carrer de S'Aigua 5. ☏ 971 713869.

La Cueva € A small but lively tapas restaurant, where hams hang from the ceiling, at the heart of La Llotja. ⊘ Carrer dels Apuntadors 5. ☏ 971 724422.

Arroceríes Ca Cranca €€ The speciality of this restaurant on the seafront is paella, freshly cooked to order and served in a number of different styles, including vegetarian.
⊘ Passeig Marítim 13. ☏ 971 737447. ⌚ 13.00–15.30, 20.00–23.30 Tues–Sat.

Baisakhi €€ A highly rated and sophisticated Indian restaurant on the seafront. ⊘ Passeig Marítim 8. ☏ 971 736806.

Casa Eduardo €€ One of the city's premier fish restaurants, located in the fishing port. ⊘ Industria Pesquera 4. ☏ 971 721182.

Giovanni's €€ Home-made pasta, tasty pizzas and other Italian dishes have made this busy restaurant popular with both locals and visitor alike. ⓐ Carrer Sant Joan 3. ⓣ 971 722879. ⓛ 13.00–15.30, 19.00–24.00 Tues–Sun.

Le Bistrot €€ Stylish French cuisine in a Parisian-style bistro. Try the sensational steak tartare. ⓐ Carrer Teodoro Llorente 4. ⓣ 971 287175.

Orient Express €€ Top-notch crêpes and tapas served in a carriage of the great Orient Express. ⓐ Carrer Llotja de Mar 6. ⓣ 971 711183.

Shogun €€ Palma's most popular Japanese restaurant, located below Bellver castle. ⓐ Carrer Camilo José Cela 14. ⓣ 971 735748. ⓝ Bus 3, 6 and 50.

Aramis €€€ Currently one of the best restaurants in Palma, with a simple, smart interior and modern Mediterranean cuisine. ⓐ Carrer Montenegro 1. ⓣ 971 725232. ⓦ www.restaurante-aramis.com ⓛ Closed Sat lunch and Sun.

Caballito de Mar €€€ Fresh fish and seafood dishes, such as sea bass baked in rock salt, are the specialities at this busy seafront restaurant. ⓐ Passeig Sagrera 5. ⓣ 971 721074. ⓛ 13.00–16.00, 20.00–24.00.

Koldo Royo €€€ Basque chef Koldo Royo's imaginative Mediterranean nouvelle cuisine and comprehensive wine list have made his eponymous restaurant on the sea promenade one of the island's finest, frequently visited by members of the Spanish royal family. ⓐ Passeig Marítim 3. ⓣ 971 732435.

Culture

Auditorium Palma's premier theatre venue, located on the waterfront and staging theatre, opera, classical concerts and ballet. ⓐ Passeig Marítim. ❶ 971 234735 (box office).

Teatre Municipal This theatre frequently features contemporary drama, classic films, dance and ballet. ⓐ Passeig Mallorca 9b. ❶ 971 739148 (box office).

Bars & nightclubs

Abaco Palma's most unusual cocktail bar is situated inside a 17th-century palace, with caged birds, fountains, candles, classical music and huge baskets of fruit. ⓐ Carrer Sant Joan 1. ❶ 971 714939. ❷ 20.00–01.30 (until 03.30 Fri–Sat).

Barbero A small, disco bar playing everything including house, jazz, funk, blues and soul. ⓐ Carrer Jaume Ferrer 3. ❷ from 23.00 Wed–Sat.

Bar Barcelona Popular with locals and tourists alike, this intimate jazz club plays live, mellow jazz nightly from 23.00 until around 03.00. ⓐ Carrer des Apuntadores 5. ❶ 971 713557.

Garito's This groovy, split-level bar attracts a young, pre-clubbing crowd and, at weekends, plays host to the hippest DJs in town, with everything from easy listening to jazz and salsa beats. ⓐ Darsena de Can Barbarà. ❷ 18.00–late.

Harbour Club By day, local yachties congregate at the cool white and turquoise poolside bar of the city's newest chill-out zone in the Club de Mar yacht club. By night, its chic terrace, lounges and bars are the latest favourite haunt of the beautiful people of Palma. Try the 'Club de Mar' cocktail. ⓐ Club de Mar, Moll Pelaires. ⓣ 971 404091. ⓦ www.harbourclubpalma.com ⓛ 09.00–24.00.

La Bodeguita del Medio A lively imitation of its Havana namesake, with Cuban rhythms, wicked daiquiris and rum-drenched mojitos. ⓐ Carrer de Vallseca 18. ⓣ 971 717832. ⓛ 22.00–03.30.

Made in Brasil Salsa the night away at this lively tropical bar, with its heady mix of caipirinas and Latin beats. ⓐ Passeig Marítim 27. ⓣ 971 454569. ⓛ 20.00–04.30.

Pacha This popular nightclub attracts a young crowd to its energetic Balearic beats. ⓐ Passeig Marítim 42. ⓣ 971 455908. ⓦ www.pachamallorca.com ⓛ 23.00–06.00.

Sazonito A cosy, candlelit cocktail bar near La Llotja, with cool beats, trendy clientele and a Mediterranean ambience. Or try their partner bar Sazon, round the corner in Carrer Apuntadores. ⓐ Carrer Jaume Ferrer 14. ⓣ 971 710587. ⓛ 19.30–01.00 (03.00 Fri–Sat).

Tito's Palma's largest, most famous and rather commercial nightclub, with six bars holding up to 2000 dancers, laser shows, house music and superb views over the bay. ⓐ Passeig Marítim, s/n. ⓣ 971 730017. ⓦ www.titosmallorca.com ⓛ 22.00–06.00.

113 This super-cool venue attracts a hip crowd to its sophisticated circular bar, comfortable chill-out spaces, funky sounds and candlelit terrace by the small harbour of Can Barbará. ⓐ Local 113, Darsena de Ca'n Barbará. ⓣ 971 ⓦ www.club113.com

The Bay of Palma

The Badia de Palma (Bay of Palma) has something for everybody –
whatever you want from your holiday, you will probably find it here.
Children will love the beaches, the caves, the waterparks and the
magic of the sea, and the adults can relax, knowing that the kids are
having fun. Those who like nothing better than lying on a beach
soaking up the sun, will definitely be spoilt for choice, while night
owls will thrive in some of the wildest party resorts.

The further you go from Palma, the deeper you get into bucket-
and-spade country, with fewer cultural sights and an increasing
number of theme parks and family attractions. The resorts are easy
to reach by local bus. They vary hugely in character from glitzy Porto
Portals and the hip new suburb of Es Molinar to Magaluf, Mallorca's
legendary nightlife capital.

SIGHTS & ATTRACTIONS

The various beaches and resorts of the Bay of Palma are fantastic
places to take all the family to escape the bustle of the city and to
soak up the sun and relax, perhaps with a picnic. Allow a whole day for
the theme parks, and also for Festival Park if you are a keen shopaholic.

Beaches

Mallorca prides itself on its beaches, which are generally very clean,
with bathwater-warm shallow water, making them safe for children
and ideal for family holidays. Palma Bay boasts some of the island's
finest beaches – from magnificent, long, sandy stretches packed
with holidaymakers to tiny deserted coves with transparent
turquoise water.

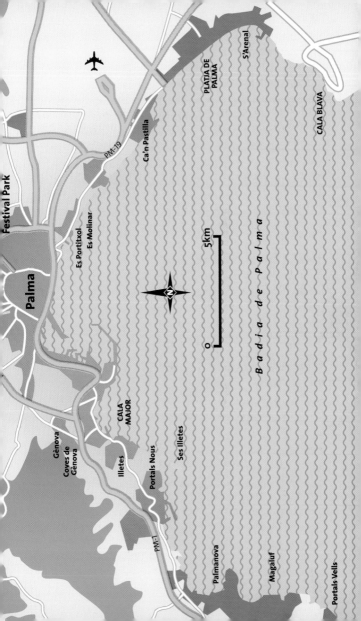

Festival Park

Palma

Gènova

Coves de Gènova

Es Portitxol

Es Molinar

Ca'n Pastilla

PLATJA DE PALMA

S'Arenal

CALA BLAVA

PM-19

Illetes

CALA MAJOR

Portals Nous

Ses Illetes

Palmanova

Magaluf

Portals Vells

PM-1

B a d i a   d e   P a l m a

N

0 ⌐ 5km ⌐

Some of the best beaches in the bay include those at the resorts of Magaluf and Palmanova and the 7 km (4 mile) stretch of sand running from Can Pastilla to S'Arenal, all of which in recent years have been given facelifts, with new promenades, imported sand and improved watersports facilities. There are also pleasant, albeit smaller, beaches at Cala Major, Illetas and Portals Nous. Alternatively, seek out one of the deserted inlets and pine-shaded *calas* (coves) indenting the wild rocky coastline south of Magaluf, including Cala Falcó, Platja Mago (popular for nude sunbathing) and Cala Portals Vells.

Coves de Gènova (Caves of Genova)

These spectacular underground caverns, with their chambers of vividly illuminated stalactites and stalagmites, can be found in the char[er]ful village of Gènova, high on the slopes of the Serra de Na Burguesa hills above Palma. Gènova itself has a surprisingly high number of traditional-style restaurants for its size, and is especially popular with Mallorcan families.

🄰 Carrer de Barranc, Gènova. ❶ 971 402387. 🕒 Apr–Oct 10.00–13.30, 16.00–19.00; Nov–Mar 10.00–13.00, 16.00–18.00. Ⓝ Bus 4. Admission charge.

Illetes

This relaxing beach resort to the west of Palma takes its name from the pair of rocky islets that can be seen just offshore. This quiet, low-key resort, with two good beaches overlooking Palma Bay, is a Spanish residential area and also a popular weekend outing for families from Palma – with the result that it is by far the most Spanish of the Bay of Palma resorts.

🄰 Carretera Andratx 33. Ⓝ Bus 3.

● *Portals Nous is the Balearics' most upmarket resort*

Porto Portals – Portals Nous

Portals Nous is the St Tropez of the Balearics and Mallorca's most glamorous holiday resort. Its glitzy harbour – Porto Portals – is considered to be the best yachting marina in the Balearics. Crammed with de luxe boutiques and fashionable restaurants and bars, it is a great venue for people-watching and celebrity-spotting. And it's also where Palma's jetset come to enjoy a night of partying out of town.

● Portals Nous. ● IB Bus 103, 104, 106, 107 or 111.

Palmanova

'New Palma', beautifully situated on a wide, sandy bay to the west of Palma, was one of Mallorca's first tourist resorts. Sandwiched between the ritzy harbour at Porto Portals and the riotous nightlife of Magaluf, it remains an excellent resort for families, with golden beaches and a wide choice of restaurants. Children especially enjoy the watersports and Golf Fantasia, one of the best mini-golf courses on the island.

Palmanova Tourist Information Office ⓐ Passeig de la Mar 13.
ⓣ 971 682365. Ⓝ IB Bus 103, 104, 105, 106 or 107.

Magaluf

Magaluf, more than anywhere else, exemplifies the rapid growth of Mallorcan tourism. What was once no more than a quiet fishing village surrounded by marshes on the western edge of Palma Bay has been transformed over the last half-century into a pulsating mega-resort, where the summer months have become one long, continuous 24-hour party.

The beach, with its long seafront promenade, is one of the best on the island, and if you fancy something more energetic than sunbathing there are canoes and pedalos for hire – as well as windsurfing and snorkelling equipment, boat trips and even a 2-hour underwater excursion in a Nemo Submarine. Children enjoy such attractions as Aqualand (see page 104) and Karting Magaluf (see page 150). But most visitors to Magaluf save their energy for the nightlife. From discos and cocktail bars to rip-roaring dinner shows and dubious 'adult entertainment', Mallorca's nightlife capital has it all.

Magaluf Tourist Information Office ⓐ Carrer Pere Vaquer Ramis 1.
ⓣ 971 131126. Ⓝ IB Bus 103, 104, 105, 106 or 107.

Ⓞ *Mallorca's original high-rise resort – Magaluf*

Marineland

A great day out for all the family. Performing dolphins, sea lions and parrots are the star turns at this sea-life centre, and there is also a penguin pool, a reptile house and an aquarium with sharks and tropical fish on display. Children have fun on the miniature train or playing in the adventure playground and the mock pirate ship.

🅐 Carrer Garcilaso de la Vega 9, Costa d'En Blanes. ☎ 971 675125.
🅦 www.marineland.es 🕒 Jan–Nov 09.30–17.00 (18.00 July–Aug).
🅝 IB Bus 103, 104, 106, 107 or 111.

Festival Park

Just 15 minutes from Palma, this spacious leisure complex provides a good day out for all the family with its enormous range of facilities and activities, including 26 different shops and factory outlets, 30 restaurants, two cinemas, 22-lane bowling, not to mention the largest reptilarium in Europe and the Mallorca Rural Museum, containing over 500 miniature model scenes of rural life and trades of the past on the island. There's even open-air evening entertainment in the centre square.

🅐 Autopista Palma-Inca, Km 7,1. ☎ 971 226822.
🅦 www.festivalpark.es 🅝 IB bus 20.

Portixol/Es Molinar

The suburb of Es Molinar and the small bay of Portixol, with its own harbour, marina and tiny beach, are within easy walking distance to the east of Palma. In the last five years this sleepy fishing district has flourished and it now boasts a beautiful promenade, a chic boutique hotel and some of the hippest restaurants in Mallorca.

🅝 Bus 15, 17 or 18.

Ca'n Pastilla & Platya de Palma

Just 5 minutes from Palma Town, these two resorts merge smoothly into one another as you stroll along the main promenade. Ideal for families, young and old, days are spent lazing on the broad sandy beach which stretches for 7 km (4 miles) as far as S'Arenal, or enjoying the various watersports on offer, including water-skiing, windsurfing and pedalo hire. At night, choose between living it up in one of the many bars and discos or enjoying a quiet meal on the seafront overlooking the beautiful bay of Palma from an array of international restaurants.

Playa de Palma Tourist Information Office ❷ Plaça Meravelles, s/sn. ❶ 971 264532. ❷ Bus 15, 17 or 23.

S'Arenal

The bustling resort of S'Arenal sits at one end of the long Platja de Palma, more than 5 km (3 miles) of wide sandy beach, with the twin resort of Ca'n Pastilla at the other end. The resorts have a highly international flavour, with English pubs, German and Dutch bars, and visitors from all over Europe converging on the beach. In the 1920s, when tourists started coming to S'Arenal, the beach was divided into sections for men, women and animals. Nowadays it is one long free-for-all – if the stretch you are on is too crowded, just move along until you find some space.

There is plenty here to keep everyone happy, with facilities for windsurfing and water-skiing as well as pedalo hire for the less adventurous. Children can splash safely around in the shallow water, and there are also a number of playgrounds spread out behind the beach. A palm-lined promenade runs the length of the resort, offering good views across Palma Bay. If you don't feel like walking, take the mini-train or go for a ride in a *galera* (horse and carriage).

S'Arenal Tourist Information Office ⓐ Plaça Reina Maria Cristina, s/n.
ⓣ 971 440414. Ⓝ Bus 15 or 23.

Aqualand, S'Arenal

Billed as the biggest waterpark in Europe, Magaluf's sister-themepark Aqualand S'Arenal has enough thrills and spills to keep children busy all day. Older children enjoy such hair-raising rides as Kamikaze and Black Hole, though fortunately there are also other, more sedate, rides for younger children. Among the many other attractions are go-karting, parrot shows, falconry demonstrations and a mini-farm.
ⓐ Palma – S'Arenal motorway, exit 13. ⓣ 971 440000.
Ⓦ www.aqualand.es/elarenal/mallorca ⓛ mid May–Sept 10.00–17.00 (18.00 July–Aug). Ⓝ Bus 23.

CULTURE

While there is much to see on the fringes of the city, the plentiful art and culture of the centre begins to dry up the further afield you go in the Bay of Palma. However, Museu Krekovic, in the eastern outskirts, is worth a visit, and the magnificent Fundació Pilar i Joan Miró, in Cala Major to the west, counts among the island's most important galleries.

Fundació Pilar i Joan Miró (Pilar and Joan Miró Gallery), Cala Major

The abstract Catalan artist Joan Miró lived on Mallorca for much of his life, and his house and studio have been turned into a museum of his work, with a fantastically modern and spacious interior, using water, concrete and light to juxtapose his splashy canvases of primary colours. The garden contains several sculptures and a café, while his studio (which opens at 11.00) has been left largely untouched since his death in 1983, with tins of paint still lying around open on the tables. The museum is in the heart of the lively, popular suburb of Cala Major, with its magnificent sandy beach, good restaurants, shops and bars. Apart from the museum, the resort's most prestigious address is Palau Marivent, a villa owned by the King of Spain.

ⓐ Carrer Joan de Saridakis 29, Cala Major. ❶ 971 701420.
🕒 10.00–18.00 (19.00 during summer months) Tues–Sat, 10.00–15.00 Sun. Admission charge. Ⓝ Bus 3 or 6.

A ROYAL ISLAND

The Spanish royal family holidays in Mallorca at least three times a year, in the aptly named Palau Marivent ('Mar i Vent' means 'Wind and Sea') – an impressive waterfront villa in Cala Major. Their visits usually coincide with major sporting events, including the Princess Sofia Cup sailing regatta at Easter and the HRH Princess Elena Horse Jumping Trophy in August.

Colección Pintor Krekovic

This small museum in Querétaro, an eastern suburb of Palma, is devoted to the romantic paintings of the Croatian artist Kristian Krekovic, who lived in Palma for the last 20 years of his life until his death in 1985. His bold-coloured paintings cover themes as diverse as the early civilisations of South America, Spanish daily life and his homeland.

ⓐ Carrer Ciutat de Querétaro 3. ❶ 971 249409. 🕒 09.30–13.00, 15.00–18.00 Mon–Fri; 09.30–13.00 Sat. Closed Aug. Admission charge. Ⓝ Bus 12 or 18.

RETAIL THERAPY

Carrefour If you are staying in self-catering accommodation, this huge hypermarket on the northern outskirts of Palma provides quick and easy one-stop shopping for your holiday. ⓐ Carrer General Riera 15 (clearly signposted from the *Via Cintura* ring road). ⓦ Bus 16.

El Corte Inglés Palma's second branch of this leading Spanish department store (see page 90), with a huge range of clothing, fashion accessories, electronics, books, toys, film processing, eateries, supermarket and underground parking. ⓐ Avinguda d'Alexandre Roselló 12. ⓣ 971 770177. ⓦ www.elcorteingles.es ⓝ All buses.

Festival Park Pick up some bargains from the likes of Levis, Reebok, Quiksilver, Nike and Mango at this huge factory outlet centre, and visit the summer crafts market (18.00–23.00 Fri–Sat) for some local souvenirs and handicrafts. ⓐ Autopista Palma-Inca, Km 7.1. ⓣ 971 226822. ⓛ 10.00–22.00 Mon–Sat; 11.00–22.00 Sun. ⓦ www.festivalpark.es ⓝ IB Bus 20.

Fundacio Pilar i Joan Miró The tiny gift shop in the basement of the Joan Miró museum has a wonderful range of unusual gifts, including arty Miró mugs and T-shirts, jewellery, books and *siurells* – clay whistles resembling a man in a hat playing a guitar or sitting on a donkey, painted white with flashes of red and green – which have been made in Mallorca and given as tokens of friendship since Arab times. Miró was said to have been much influenced by their brightness and simplicity. ⓐ Carrer Joan de Saridakis 29, Cala Major. ⓣ 971 701420. ⓛ 10.00–18.00 (19.00 during summer months) Tues–Sat, 10.00–15.00 Sun. ⓝ Bus 3 or 6.

Porto Pi The massive Porto Pi hypermarket-cum-shopping centre at the western end of the Passeig Marítim has over 100 shops under one roof, including fashion boutiques, delicatessens, eateries and ice-cream parlours, gifts and handicraft shops, and a safe play area for children. 🅐 Passeig Marítim. 🕐 10.00–22.00 Mon–Sat. Ⓝ Bus 1, 14 or 50.

Blue Willi's One of several upmarket boutiques in Porto Portals, Blue Willi's pride themselves on producing high-quality casual yet stylish clothes made from pure natural materials and dyed with indigo. 🅐 Porto Portals. 🕿 971 676426. Ⓝ IB bus 103, 104, 106, 107 or 111.

TAKING A BREAK

Many of the bars and restaurants in the 'After Dark' section (see page 110) also serve food and drinks during the day.

Flanigan Join yachties at this Porto Portals institution for a hearty breakfast or the house speciality – apple tart. 🅐 Porto Portals, Portals Nous. 🕿 971 679191. Ⓝ IB bus 103, 104, 106, 107 or 111.

Minimar Trendy white-on-white minimalist tapas bar in a prime location on the seafront at Portixol. Fish and shellfish predominate. 🅐 Carrer Vicari Joaquin Fuster 67, Portixol. 🕿 971 248604. Ⓝ Bus 15, 17 or 18.

Tahini Taste the freshest of fish at this sophisticated sushi bar with its very own bamboo garden. 🅐 Porto Portals. 🕿 971 676025. Ⓝ IB bus 103, 104, 106, 107 or 111.

Diablito A popular waterfront pizzeria overlooking the ostentatious boats in the Porto Portals marina. Try the 'Popeye' pizza or 'The Sailor's Favourite'! ❷ Porto Portals. ❶ 971 676503.
ⓦ www.diablitofoodandmusic.com ❷ IB bus 103, 104, 106, 107 or 111.

AFTER DARK

From traditional Mallorquin cuisine in old-fashioned country restaurants to fine fish in trendy minimalist seafront cafés, the Bay of Palma has it all. It also enjoys some of the finest nightlife on the island, embracing the newly fashionable suburb of Portixol/Es Molinar, the upmarket night haunts of Porto Portals, two major new beach party venues, lively theme evenings, and the tourist-touting mega-disco BCM in the notorious resort of Magaluf.

Restaurants

Ca'n Pedro € Snails are a speciality at this traditional-style restaurant, with its hearty Mallorquin cooking. ❷ Carrer de Rector Vives 14, Gènova. ❶ 971 402479. ❷ Bus 4.

Rocamar €€ A top-notch fish and seafood restaurant, with black minimalist decor and a stylish terrace, frequented by Palma's smart set. ❷ Carrer Vicario Joaquin Fuster 1, Portixol. ❶ 971 274644. ❷ Bus 15, 17 or 18.

Samantha's €€€ For that special occasion, dine in style in a traditional villa in Bonanova, overlooking the Bay of Palma and Bellver Castle. The Mediterranean cuisine is sensational and there is also an impressive wine list. ❷ Carrer Francesc Vidal i Sureda 115. ❶ 971 700000. ❷ Bus 6.

Bars & nightclubs

Abacanto A sophisticated cocktail bar in a lavish mansion in the suburb of Indioteria – the country version of Palma's exotic Abaco bar (see page 96) ❸ Camino de Son Nicolau, s/n, Indoteria. ❶ 971 430624. ❼ www.abacanto.es ❿ Bus 10.

BCM One of Europe's largest discos, with spectacular laser shows, swimming pool, foam parties and big-name DJs. ❸ Avinguda S'Olivera, s/n, Magaluf. ❶ 971 132609. ❼ www.bcm-planetdance.com ❿ IB bus 103, 104, 105, 106 or 107.

Kaskai An ultra-cool bar despite its cosy red interior, on the seafront at Es Molinar, with tables spilling out onto the pavement. The perfect setting for *una copa romantica*. ❸ Carrer Vicario Joaquin Fuster 71, Portixol. ❶ 971 241284. ❸ Closed Wed. ❿ Bus 15, 17 or 18.

Portals Nous Join Palma's jetset for a night out of town in Porto Portals. Late-night bars **Havana Moon** (Locale 30), **Zebra** (Locale 57) and **Bar del Titanic** (Locale 45) are currently the 'in' places to see and be seen. ❸ Porto Portals. ❿ IB bus 103, 104, 106, 107 or 111.

Puro Beach The latest addition to the party scene, this new beach- and poolside bar venue near the airport draws the beautiful people of Palma by day for yoga, cocktails and chilling out, but by night it comes alive for vibrant sunset parties with resident DJs playing all the latest Balearic beats. ❸ Carrer Pagell 12. ❶ 971 744744. ❼ www.purobeach.com

Virtual Club Think of this as a funky Flintstones experience! This sophisticated beach club by day dissolves into a beach party by sundown, with a spectacular bar set in natural caves, and music throughout the night. ⓐ Passeig d'Illetes 60. ① 971 703235. ⓦ www.virtualclub.es ⓒ 12.00–02.00. ⓝ Bus 3.

Cinema and entertainment
Ocimax
This leisure centre on the outskirts of Palma has 15 cinema screens (with a few films in English), 26-lane bowling and a wide choice of restaurants and bars, a great venue on a rainy day. ⓐ Carretera Valldemossa, s/n. ① 971 750673. ⓝ Bus 12.

Pirate's Adventure A great family night out, with a swashbuckling pirates adventure show. Audience participation is encouraged, with free-flowing Pirate Punch to loosen your inhibitions. Booking is strongly advised. ⓐ Carretera de sa Porrassa. ① 971 130411. ⓒ Family show at 18.00 and 20.00; adult show at 21.00 and 23.00. ⓝ IB bus 103, 104, 105, 106 or 107.

Son Amar A fun, spectacular, all-singing and all-dancing late-night show, in a converted 16th-century mansion, with cabaret, flamenco, magicians and live bands, a 10-minute drive north of Palma. Ask the tourist office or your holiday rep for details of coach excursions. ⓐ Carretera de Soller Km 10, Bunyola. ① 971 617533. ⓦ www.sonamar.com

▶ *Fornalutx is regarded as one of Spain's prettiest villages*

OUT OF TOWN
trips

Valldemossa & Deià

The north-western coastline contains some of the most spectacular scenery on Mallorca, with pine-scented forests and terraced hillsides tumbling into the sea. This corner of Mallorca has long appealed to foreigners – Frédéric Chopin and Robert Graves were both drawn here, and Michael Douglas and Andrew Lloyd Webber have homes in the area today. Hire a car (or ask your holiday rep about daytrips) to visit the 'celebrity' mountain villages of Deià and Valldemossa and the surrounding countryside, to see the best that the region has to offer.

SIGHTS & ATTRACTIONS

Valldemossa

Valldemossa is one of the best-known villages in Mallorca, and is located just 15 km (10 miles) north of Palma in the Tramuntana mountains. Here Frédéric Chopin and his mistress, the French authoress George Sand, spent the winter of 1838–39 in the Reial Cartoixa (Carthusian monastery). The monastery and scenery have changed little since, and Valldemossa remains well worth visiting if only for the monastic peace after the bustle of Mallorca's beach resorts.

Chopin and Sand came to Mallorca to escape the gossip of Paris, and hoping that the mild climate would improve Chopin's ill health. However, Chopin's piano failed to arrive, his health deteriorated and so did their relationship. Afterwards, Sand wrote an angry book in which she described the Mallorcans as thieves and monkeys. Valldemossa is also the birthplace of the island's patron saint, Santa Catalina Tomás, and nearly every house in the village has a painted

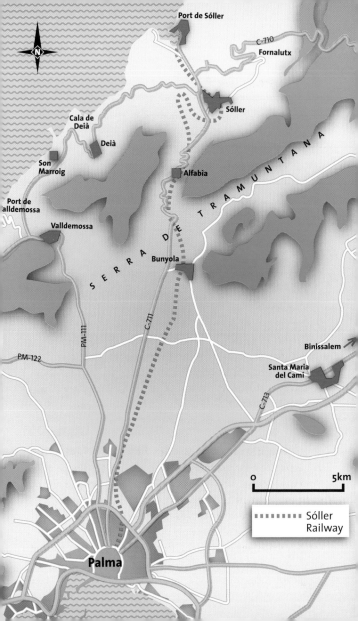

tile beside the front door asking for the saint's protection. Today, it is better known as the second home of Hollywood royalty Michael Douglas and Catherine Zeta-Jones. Douglas has owned a country estate here for over 20 years. He has recently sponsored a new cultural centre in the village, Costa Nord, which hosts frequent concerts and during the day shows a documentary recounting the history of this region, narrated by Douglas himself.

Celebrities past and present have chosen Deià as their Mediterranean hideaway

CELEBRITY ISLAND

Michael Douglas and Catherine Zeta-Jones are not the only celebrities to grace Mallorca. The island boasts an impressive guest list of luminaries among its residents, including Claudia Schiffer, Boris Becker, Annie Lennox, Andrew Lloyd Webber and Tom Cruise, and a whole host of A-list holidaymakers, including Joan Collins, Michael Schumacher, Jack Nicholson, Pierce Brosnan, Gwyneth Paltrow, Sting, Ruby Wax, Bob Geldof and Rod Stewart, who are all regular visitors to the island.

Port de Valldemossa

If you are brave enough to negotiate the 6 km (4 mile) helter-skelter drive that separates Valldemossa from its coastal port, you will enjoy numerous dramatic viewpoints and hair-raising hairpin bends before entering the charming fishing village of Port de Valldemossa. Here you will discover a handful of stone cottages, fishing boats and a small stony beach – perfect for a light lunch and a swim, before setting off again up the corkscrew road.

Deià

The artists' village of Deià is a tiny cluster of ochre-coloured houses in the shadow of the Teix mountain, just a 25-minute drive north of Palma. It was put on the map by the author and poet Robert Graves, who lived here from the 1930s until his death in 1985. He is buried beneath a simple hand-inscribed tombstone outside the church of Sant Joan Bautista at the top of the village. Deià has become a magnet for foreign artists over the last few decades, and the village

is full of small art galleries, cafés and chic hotels. Having explored, you may wish to take a drink or a meal at La Residencia, which used to belong to Richard Branson – but be warned, it is very pricey. Centrally located, this five-star hotel (see page 127) is set back off the main Deià road in beautiful terraced gardens.

Cala de Deià

Just a 30-minute stroll from Deià, this tiny pebbly cove with its jagged cliffs and icy, clear waters is one of the hidden gems of Mallorca's north coast. There is even a ramshackle beach bar and a restaurant, Sa Caleta, for refreshments.

Lafiore Glass Factory

Glass has been made on the island since Roman times and glass-making techniques have changed little since then. Here you can watch crafts people at work in the glass-blowing workshop, before visiting the extensive shop next door where jugs, vases, drinking glasses and candleholders are the most popular buys. ❷ Carretera de Valldemossa, Km 11, S'Esgleieta. ● 09.15–20.00 Mon–Fri, 09.15–13.00, 15.00–18.00 Sat.

CULTURE

La Cartoixa (The Charterhouse)

Visit the Carthusian monastery – the second most visited site on the island (after Palma's cathedral) – to see the monk's cell where Frédéric Chopin and George Sand stayed, as well as the old pharmacy and an excellent museum of modern art including work

● *The Charterhouse of Valldemossa has attracted visitors since Chopin's time*

by Picasso and Miró. There are regular recitals of Chopin's music and you can even buy a copy of Sand's book. ❶ 971 612106. ⓦ www.valldemossa.com/cartu.htm ⏱ Mar–Oct 09.30–18.00 Mon–Sat, 10.00–13.00 Sun; Nov–Feb 09.30–16.30 Mon–Sat. Admission charge.

Son Marroig

Perched high above the north coast between Valldemossa and Deià, with stunning sea views, this mansion was once the home of Mallorca's greatest admirer, the wealthy Austrian aristocrat and ecologist Archduke Luis Salvador. Known to the locals simply as S'Arxiduc, he spent the best part of his life here studying and recording Mallorcan wildlife and traditions. Today his house is open to the public, providing a fascinating insight into island life in bygone years. The garden contains a graceful white-marble rotunda where the Archduke would sit and contemplate the sea, the mountains and Sa Foradada – a remarkable rocky headland jutting out to sea with a massive hole at its centre. ⓐ Carretera Deià–Valldemossa. ⏱ 10.00–19.00 Mon–Sat (until 17.00 in winter months). Admission charge.

La Granja

If time permits, it's worth making a detour to see one of Mallorca's finest country houses, originally constructed by the Cistercians as a monastery, which has since been turned into a fascinating open-air museum of rural life and traditions. The best time to visit is during the 'folk fiesta' on Wednesday and Friday afternoons, when folk dancers perform in the courtyard and women in traditional

---

▶ The Archduke's gazebo at Son Marroig

costume give displays of lace-making and embroidery. There are free
tastings of cheese and sausages, doughnuts and fig-cake, and the
restaurant serves up typical Mallorcan fare. The tour of the house
includes the family chapel, the medieval kitchens – and a dungeon
with a torture chamber! ⓐ Carretera Esporles– Puigpunyent, Km 2,
Esporles. ⓘ 971 610032. ⓛ 10.00–19.00. Admission charge.

Deià Archaeological Museum

Small, fascinating museum, worth visiting for the extremely attractive
conversion of an old mill and prehistoric finds from nearby caves.
ⓐ Es Clot, Deià. ⓘ 971 639001. ⓛ 17.00–19.00 Tues, Thur and Sun.

RETAIL THERAPY

There are plenty of souvenir, arts and handicraft shops in
Valldemossa and Deià, selling fine handmade pottery, glass,
jewellery, woodwork and table linen.

Valldemossa
Bodega Delicatessen This smart shop on the outskirts of the village
specialises in Mallorcan wines, together with a small selection of
locally produced jams, preserves, oils and nougat. ⓐ Carrer Sor Aina
Cirer. ⓘ 971 616355. ⓦ www.sabodega.com

Cals Tios Brightly coloured shoes, funky handbags and clothing and
chunky costume jewellery, all made in Mallorca. ⓐ Carrer Blanqueria
15c. ⓘ 971 612615.

● *Picturesque Valldemossa – a great place to escape from the city and hunt
for souvenirs*

Ponent A treasure trove of fine gifts and souvenirs, from olive oil, *sobrasada* sausages and locally produced marmalade to hand-carved olivewood, ceramics and glassware.
🅐 Carrer Blanqueria 15c.

Souvenirs Catalina Calafat This jam-packed shop sells everything from Lladro, lace and leatherware to *siurells* (see page 22) and replica Chopin pianos. 🅐 Plaça Cartoixa 1. 🕿 971 612461.

Deià
Alic A tiny studio selling high-quality handmade ceramics and jewellery. 🅐 Carrer Porxo 5. 🕿 971 639330. 🕒 11.00–13.30, 16.00–20.00. Closed most Sat afternoons and Sun.

Arte This artisan's workshop sells unusual pottery, glass and olivewood utensils. 🅐 Plaça de la Iglesia 2. 🕿 971 639126. 🕒 11.00–13.30, 15.00–19.00 (except Sat afternoon and Sun).

Forn Deià Ca Na Margalida The village store is a fantastic one-stop store for all your picnic needs. 🅐 Carrer Arxiduc Lluis Salvador, Deià. 🕒 11.00–13.30, 16.00–20.00 (except Sat afternoon and Sun).

Taller de Joanna A tiny potter's workshop, crammed full of rustic dishes, tiles and door plaques. 🅐 Deià. 🕿 971 639384.

TAKING A BREAK

Don't leave Valldemossa without having tried the local delicacies – *coca de patates* (light, fluffy buns dusted in icing sugar) – washed down with a chilled *horchata de almendra* (almond milkshake).

Valldemossa

Es Port Set in Valldemossa's isolated fishing village, this small restaurant serves the freshest of fish and massive paellas.
ⓐ Port de Valldemossa. ☎ 971 616194. ⏱ 13.00–15.30, 20.00–22.30.

Meriendas This cheap, cheerful locals' café serves sandwiches, cakes, pizzas and wickedly rich *xocolate* (hot chocolate).
ⓐ Carrer Blanquera. ⏱ 08.00–20.00.

Deià

Sa Caleta Grilled squid, prawns and swordfish are the specialities in this beachside restaurant, perched high on the cliffs overlooking a picturesque cove.
ⓐ Cala de Deià. ☎ 971 639137. ⏱ 11.00–19.00.

Xelini This cellar-style bar with stone floors serves a fantastic spread of tapas laid along a huge bar – everything from tortilla and shrimps to sobrasada, octopus and stuffed peppers.
ⓐ Carrer Arxiduc Lluis Salvador 19. ☎ 971 639139. ⓦ www.xelini.com

AFTER DARK

Restaurants

Ca'n Pedro €€ A large, atmospheric cellar restaurant on the edge of the village, serving hearty Mallorcan fare.
ⓐ Carrer Arxiduc Lluis Salvador, Valldemossa. ☎ 971 612170.
⏱ 13.00–16.00, 19.00–23.00 (daily except Sun night & Mon).

Jaume €€ Mallorcan cuisine – *tumbet*, *sopes mallorquines*, *bacalao* (salt cod), etc – in a simple yet stylish dining room with a terrace

OUT OF TOWN

overlooking the village and the valley.
🄰 Carrer Arxiduc Lluis Salvador 22, Deià. 🕿 971 639029.

Sa Cartoixa €€ *Tumbet*, rabbit stew and paella are the specialities in
this bustling café-restaurant right at the heart of the village.
🄰 Plaça Ramòn Llull 5, Valldemossa. 🕿 971 616059. 🕒 08.00–23.00.

El Olivo €€€ Top-notch nouvelle cuisine in a converted oil-mill,
attached to Hotel La Residencia. 🄰 Carrer Son Canals, s/n, Deià.
🕿 971 639011.

Bars
Albar This cool new bar in Deià draws a hip crowd to its comfy sofas
and modish interiors for late-night drinking, and occasional live
music. 🄰 Carrer Arxiduc Lluis Salvador 9, Deià. 🕿 971 636098.
🕒 Most nights until 03.00.

ACCOMMODATION

Valldemossa

Ca'n Mário € A simple budget hotel in the heart of the village, with just 16 rooms and a popular restaurant. ⓐ Carrer de Uetam 8. ⓣ 971 612122.

Deià

Villa Verde € A surprisingly affordable pension in the centre of Deià, with a beautiful terrace overlooking the village. ⓐ Carrer Ramon Llull 19. ⓣ 971 639037.

La Residencia €€€ Mallorca's top country hotel, formerly owned by Richard Branson, with every imaginable home comfort. ⓐ Carrer Son Canals, s/n. ⓣ 971 639011. ⓦ www.hotel-laresidencia.com

⬇ *Taking it easy at La Residencia*

Palma to Port de Sóller – the Mountain Express

The old-fashioned toytown train ride from Palma to Sóller is one of the highlights of any visit to Mallorca. The guards with their whistles, and the vintage carriages with their polished mahogany and brass panels, conjure up an image of a bygone age of travel. The 27 km (16 mile) journey takes about an hour. At the end of it all is a joyride down to the sea, in an antique tram imported from San Francisco.

The railway line, cut through the mountains in 1912, opened up Mallorca's previously inaccessible northern coastline to day trippers from Palma. The tram service started the following year, and soon Port de Sóller became a fashionable resort. Nowadays the 'Mountain Express' is a must on every visitor's itinerary – with the result that the trains get very crowded at peak times. Six trains a day make the return journey from Palma, but unless you are a keen photographer, you can escape the worst of the crowds by avoiding the 10.50 and 12.15 *turistico* trains, which make an extra stop at a scenic viewpoint overlooking Sóller.

SIGHTS & ATTRACTIONS

Visitors who travel by train will arrive at the main station at the heart of Sóller, near the tourist office, so many of the top sights are only a short walk away. Sóller is well worth exploring for a couple of hours before departing for Port de Sóller. If you come by car from Palma, parking in one of Sóller's central car parks is easy, and it gives you the flexibility to visit some of the other attractions in the area,

● *The Sóller train spends a magic hour travelling through the mountains*

including the picturesque mountain village of Fornalutx and the lush gardens of Alfàbia.

Bunyola

The train rattles through Palma's poorer suburbs and out onto the pancake-flat plain, passing almond and orange groves before climbing to the hill village of Bunyola. If you want to break your journey, you can get off here to explore this pretty village and to visit the Tunel factory, where many of Mallorca's herb-based liqueurs are made. Be sure to try the *palo*, a sweet, carob-based liqueur.

Tunel ⓐ Carrer Vinyetes, Bunyola.

Sóller

The friendly market town of Sóller, nestling in the lush Valley of Oranges at the heart of the Serra de Tramuntana mountains, never fails to captivate its many visitors, thanks to the cool climate, the crisp mountain air, the traditional lifestyle, the architecture and the culinary delights – not forgetting the excellent shopping facilities.

Sóller had its heyday in the 19th century, with the production of olive oil and the export of oranges and lemons to the South of France directly from Port de Sóller. The influences of this flourishing trade can be seen today in the lovely manor houses and surrounding farmsteads whose facades show an elegance unusual for this type of rural building in Mallorca. Ca'n Prunera mansion, in Carrer Sa Lluna, and the Bank of Sóller, with its fancy wrought-ironwork, in Plaça Constitució, are just two examples. Today, Sóller is a delightful place to soak up the atmosphere of an authentic Mallorcan town, to enjoy a lazy lunch, or to potter about the

---

● *Sóller's architecture is surprisingly sophisticated for a small market town*

> ### THE ORANGE BLIGHT
> Situated in the broad, fertile Valle de los Naranjos (Valley of the Oranges), Sóller is redolent of the 19th century, when its residents grew prosperous from the local fruit trade. However, in the 1860s the orange groves were struck by blight, and many of Sóller's citizens were forced to seek their fortunes elsewhere. Many emigrated to mainland Europe in search of work. When they returned they brought with them new and fanciful ideas, including *Modernista* architecture.

traditional-style shops. And be sure to spend some time in the main square, Plaça Constitució – a pleasant place to sit and watch the trams, with their open-sided carriages, trundling past the church en route to picturesque Port de Sóller just a 30-minute ride away.

Port de Sóller

The Orange Express trams from Sóller to its port leave every half hour (07.00–20.00) from the station and the main square, passing through orchards of citrus fruit on their way down to the sea. The two beaches at Port de Sóller are the only sandy ones along the entire northern coast until Cala Sant Vicenç to the north. The main beach runs beside the tramway. The second beach – Platja d'en Repic – fronts an attractive pedestrian promenade and is usually quieter. Both have sun beds, parasols and pedalos for hire, and there is also a windsurfing school. Alternatively, wander up to the lighthouse for scenic views of the port or enjoy a long lunch at one of the seafront restaurants. If you have time you can even take a cruise around the north coast from here.

Boat trips

Some of the finest views of Port de Sóller and the Serra de Tramuntana mountains beyond can only be seen from the sea. Hop on a pleasure cruise to admire the dramatic coastline, and remember your camera!

Serra de Tramuntana

Visible from all over Mallorca, the 'Mountains of the North Wind' stretch along the entire north-west coast and provide some of the island's most dramatic scenery. In winter they act as a buffer, shielding the central plain from the fierce *tramuntana* wind and absorbing much of the island's rain and snow. In summer, they provide a cool retreat from the heat of Palma and the frenetic resorts of the south.

Alfàbia

Just a couple of kilometres from Sóller, the cool, fragrant gardens of Alfàbia (from *al fabi* meaning 'jar of olives' in Arabic) are a delightful memento of times past when Mallorca was under Moorish rule. With shaded walkways and gently splashing fountains, it is an ideal spot for an afternoon siesta.

ⓐ Carretera Palma–Sóller (at the entrance to the Sóller tunnel).
ⓘ 971 613123. ⓛ May–Oct 09.30–18.30 Mon–Fri, 09.30–13.00 Sat; Nov–Apr 09.30–17.30 Mon–Fri, 09.30–13.00 Sat. Admission charge.

Fornalutx

Fornalutx claims to be the most beautiful village in all Spain, set in a valley of citrus groves with Puig Major, the highest mountain on the island, as its backdrop. Its honey-coloured houses and steep cobbled streets dotted with café terraces are a joy to explore.

CULTURE

Museu de Sóller

If you are interested in the history of the town, this delightful 18th-century manor house crammed with relics of old Sóller is worth a visit. ⊙ Casa de Cultura, Carrer de Sa Mar 11. ❶ 971 634663. ⏱ 11.00–17.00 Mon; 10.00–18.00 Tues–Fri; 10.00–14.00 Sat.

Museu de la Mar

This small museum in the fishermen's quarter of Port de Sóller tells the fascinating story of the people of Sóller over the centuries, from piracy and ship-building to the orange blight and the arrival of *Modernista* architecture.
⊙ Oratori de Santa Caterina d'Alexandria, Port de Sóller.
❶ 971 630200. ⏱ summer 10.00–14.00, 17.00–20.00 Tues–Sat, 10.00–14.00 Sun; winter 10.00–13.30, 15.00–18.00 Tues–Sat, 10.00–14.00 Sun.

RETAIL THERAPY

Sóller offers some of the island's best shopping outside Palma, with its numerous boutiques and craft shops. Stock up on fresh produce for a picnic on the beach at the daily covered market on Carrer Cristòfol Colom, or at the open-air market in Plaça del Mercat on Saturdays from 08.00–13.00. As in Palma, most shops are closed Saturday afternoons and on Sunday.

Ben Calçat Small shoe-manufacturer specialising in traditional Balearic footwear. ⊙ Carrer Sa Lluna 74, Sóller. ❶ 971 632874.

Ca'n Oliver This fabric shop sells the distinctive Mallorca *roba de llengües* – durable cotton cloth with colourful stripey red, green or blue patterns, commonly used on the island for curtains, bedspreads, wall furnishings, tableware and upholstery. 🄰 Carrer Lluna 25, Sóller. 🄸 971 638205.

Eugenio A treasure trove of Mallorcan pearls, fans and olive-wood souvenirs. 🄰 Carrer Jerónimo Estades 11-A, Sóller. 🄸 971 630984.

TAKING A BREAK

The open-air cafés and tapas bars of Plaça Constitució are a great place to soak up the atmosphere of Sóller. Sample the local orange and lemon juice, freshly squeezed while you wait. For those with a sweet tooth, other local specialities include ice cream and pastries.

Pasteleria Ses Delicies Be sure to taste their mouth-watering plum cake and tartaleta manzana (tarts made from local citrus fruits). 🄰 Plaça Constitució 12, Sóller. 🄸 971 630269. 🄻 10.00–19.00 Mon–Sat.

Sa Fàbrica de Gelats Children love to visit the small ice cream factory in the centre of town, well-known for its creamy ices made with the valley's famous oranges and lemons. 🄰 Avinguda Cristòfol Colom 13, Sóller. 🄸 971 631708.

Bar Es Firo Try the hearty country-style tapas here – the lamb with peppers and aubergines, fish in chilli and garlic, and snails with wild mushrooms are especially delicious. 🄰 Plaça Constitució 10b, Sóller. 🄸 971 630134. 🄻 Daily 08.00–22.00.

Es Planet Soak up the sun and the atmosphere on the pavement terrace of this popular café in the main square. It's one of the best places to try a glass of freshly squeezed orange or lemon juice.
🅐 Plaça Constitucio 3, Sóller. 🕒 Mon–Sat 07.00–21.00.

AFTER DARK

Restaurants
El Guia € An old-fashioned restaurant serving staple Mallorcan cuisine. The *menu del día* is always excellent value. 🅐 Carrer Castanyer 3, Sóller. 🕾 971 630227. 🕒 Daily 13.00–15.00, 20.00–22.00.

Café Med €€ A small restaurant just off the main square in Fornalutx, serving sophisticated international cuisine in simple, rustic surroundings. 🅐 Carrer sa Plaça 7, Fornalutx. 🕾 971 630900.
🕒 Sun–Fri, evenings only.

Es Faro €€ Enjoy 'The Lighthouse's' delicious fish dishes, served on a terrace high above the port, affording exceptional coastal views.
🅐 Carretera Faro, Cap Gros de Muleta, Port de Sóller. 🕾 971 633752.
🕒 Daily 13.00–16.00, 19.00–23.00.

Lua €€ A tiny, chic restaurant in the fishermen's quarter, perched high above the port, with exceptional views, fine wines and the freshest of fish. 🅐 Carrer Santa Catalina 1, Port de Sóller. 🕾 971 634745.

Sa Cova €€ This restaurant on Sóller's main square serves standard international cuisine as well as Mallorcan specialities, such as rabbit

◀ *The restaurants in Port de Sóller offer some of the best seafood on the island*

137

with garlic. ② Plaça Constitució 7, Sóller. ❶ 971 633222.
🕐 13.00–15.00, 19.00–22.30 Tues–Sun.

Ses Porxeres €€ Located inside a high-ceilinged barn beside the gardens of Alfàbia, this restaurant is renowned throughout the island for its game dishes. The wild boar and pheasant dishes are particularly recommended. ② Carretera Palma-Sóller (at the entrance to the Sóller tunnel), Alfàbia. ❶ 971 613762.
🕐 13.30–15.30, 20.30–23.00, daily except Sun evenings and Mon.

Entertainment

Altamar Discoteca The biggest and best disco in Sóller, playing a variety of music to appeal to all ages. ❷ Passeig Es Traves, Port de Sóller. 🕒 Mid-June-Sept 21.00–06.00 nightly; Oct–mid-June open only Fri and Sat nights.

Asgard Pub This Irish bar on the waterfront attracts a young, lively crowd for late-night drinking.
❷ Passeig Es Traves, 1, Port de Sóller.

⬇ *Port de Sóller has thriving nightlife*

Son Amar Mallorca's top nightspot, with spectacular live cabaret, near Bunyola. ⓐ Carretera de Sóller, Km 10, Bunyola. ① 971 617533. ⓦ www.sonamar.com

ACCOMMODATION

Sóller

El Guia € This traditional hotel is excellent value, conveniently located near the old railway station, and an ideal base for exploring the region. ⓐ Carrer Castanyer 3. ① 971 630227.

Hotel Salvia €€€ A beautifully renovated 18th-century townhouse at the heart of the town, with just six rooms and beautiful citrus-scented gardens (and no children under 14). ⓐ Carrer de la Palma 18. ① 971 634936.

Port de Sóller

Aimia €€ Located just one street back from the beach, everything about this chic modern hotel is designed for comfort and relaxation – minimalist rooms, friendly staff, a stylish decked pool area, a spa and a contemporary restaurant and cocktail bar (open to non-residents), which are currently the 'in' places in the port to see and be seen. ⓐ Carrer Santa Maria del Camí 1. ① 971 631200. ⓦ www.aimiahotel.com

Fornalutx

Ca'n Reus €€ A charming small hotel, popular with walkers, with nine rooms and a pretty garden, pool and terrace overlooking citrus groves and the mountains. ⓐ Carrer de l'Auba 26. ① 971 631174. ⓦ www.canreushotel.com

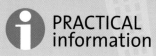

Directory

GETTING THERE

The cheapest way to get to Mallorca is to book a package holiday with one of the leading tour operators specialising in Spanish or Balearic holidays. If your travelling times are flexible, and if you can avoid the school holidays, you can also find some very cheap last-minute deals using the websites of the leading holiday companies. The Palma Town Council has a useful website, Ⓦ www.a-palma.es. Or, if you enter Mallorca (or the alternative spelling, Majorca) in any search engine, you will find a wealth of pages on every aspect – hotels, attractions, watersports, golf, restaurants, etc., in English.

By air

Iberia, the Spanish national airline, is the main operator of scheduled flights to Palma from mainland Spain and Europe, but Palma airport is also well served by charter flights from most major European cities too. For independent travellers, there are several no-frills airlines to consider too. Flights from the UK take 2–2¹/₂ hours to reach Palma. Information and online reservations can be made through the websites of leading airlines and tour operators.

Air Europa ❶ (UK) 0870 7777709, (Palma) 971 221686.
Ⓦ www.aireuropa.com
British Airways ❶ (UK) 0870 8509850, (Spain) 902 111333.
Ⓦ www.britishairways.com
British Midland ❶ (UK) 0870 6070555, (Spain) 902 999262.
Ⓦ www.britishmidland.com
EasyJet ❶ (Palma) 971 490307. Ⓦ www.easyjet.com
Iberia ❶ (UK) 0870 6090500, (Palma) 971 789980.
Ⓦ www.iberia.com

Thomsonfly ⓘ (UK) 0870 1900737. Ⓦ www.thomsonfly.com

Visitors from the USA and other continents need to take a connecting flight from the UK or other European airport.

By road

The usual route by car involves driving down through France and across the Pyrenees to Barcelona (allow not less than two days), where you can catch the daily car ferry. The journey from London to Barcelona by coach takes around 26 hours. Contact Eurolines for further information.

Eurolines ⓘ (UK) 08705 143219. Ⓦ www.eurolines.com

By rail

It takes just 15 hours by train from London via the Channel Tunnel to Barcelona, from where there are regular ferries to Palma. Contact Rail Europe for further information. The monthly *Thomas Cook European Rail Timetable* has up-to-date schedules for European international and national train and ferry services.

Rail Europe Ⓦ www.raileurope.com
Thomas Cook European Rail Timetable ⓘ (UK) 01733 416477; (USA) 1 800 322 3834. Ⓦ www.thomascookpublishing.com

By sea

There are regular ferry services connecting Palma to Barcelona, Valencia and Dénia on the Spanish mainland, as well as to the Balearic Islands of Menorca and Ibiza. Contact the operators Trasmediterránea and Balearia for further information.

Trasmediterránea Ⓦ www.trasmediterranea.com
Balearia Ⓦ www.balearia.com

ENTRY FORMALITIES

Documentation

Citizens of EU countries, USA, Canada, Australia, New Zealand and Japan who hold valid passports do not need a visa to visit Spain for less than 90 days. Other visitors should check with their nearest Spanish consulate.

Customs

Visitors to Mallorca from within the EU are entitled to bring their personal effects and goods for personal consumption and not for resale, up to a total of 800 cigarettes and 10 litres of spirits. Duty-free limits for those entering from outside the EU are 200 cigarettes (or 100 cigarillos or 50 cigars or 250g of tobacco), 1 litre of spirits (or 2 litres of fortified wines or sparkling wine) and 2 litres of wine.

MONEY

Spain's currency is the euro, with notes issued in denominations of 5, 10, 20, 50 and 100 euros, and coins of 1 and 2 euros and also 1, 2, 5, 10, 20 and 50 cents. Credit cards are widely used in Palma (especially American Express, Visa and MasterCard), but it is a good idea to carry cash to use in shops, bars and cafés, and to check the payment methods available before you order a meal or run up a bar bill. If you do get caught short, there are numerous bureaux de change in Palma and most UK banks' cash cards can be used to obtain cash in local currency from some ATMs, although the commission charged can be expensive.

HEALTH, SAFETY & CRIME

The water in Palma is generally safe to drink, although it is heavily chlorinated and not to everyone's taste. Bottled water is cheap to buy and is preferable, either still (*agua sin gas*) or carbonated (*agua con gas*). A change of diet could lead to tummy upsets, so carry a supply of anti-diarrhoea tablets. Most restaurants offer plenty of choice to suit all tastes from Mallorcan specialities to more 'international' cuisine, but vegetarians will find menus heavily meat-biased.

Thanks to a reciprocal healthcare agreement, nationals of EU countries and some other countries can get reduced-price, sometimes free, medical treatment in Spain on presentation of a valid European Health Insurance Card (EHIC), the replacement for the E111 (which ceased to be valid on 31 December 2005). This card gives access to state-provided medical treatment only. Apply online for an EHIC at Ⓦ www.dh.gov.uk/travellers and allow at least 2–3 weeks until you receive the card. On top of this, private medical insurance is still advised and is essential for all non-EU visitors. Dental treatment is not available free of charge, as Mallorcan dental practices are private, and should be covered by private medical insurance.

The biggest health hazards for visitors are sunstroke, dehydration and alcoholic over-indulgence. People who are not used to the sun burn easily, and children are especially vulnerable. It is a good idea to cover up with a strong sunblock, to wear a hat and to keep out of the midday sun by taking a siesta in the shade. Remember also to drink alcohol in moderation and plenty of bottled water.

If you need to consult a doctor (*medico*) or a dentist (*dentista*), ask for help at your hotel reception. Prescription and non-prescription medicines are available from pharmacies (*farmàcias*), indicated by a large green cross, and there is an extensive network

of health centres (*centres de salut*), which provide medical advice.
A list of pharmacies open out of hours is shown in all pharmacy
windows and published in the *Majorca Daily Bulletin*. Alternatively,
dial 11888 for information on all-night pharmacies. (For information
on medical emergencies, see page 156.)

Crime rates are low in Palma, although it is advisable to take
commonsense precautions against petty crime (see page 49), and
remember that thefts can be carried out by your fellow holidaymakers too! If you need a police station, ask for *la comisaría*. You
may see two types of police around the town: the city police or
Policia Municipal wear blue and keep the traffic under control, while
the Policia Nacional wear brown and uphold law and order.

OPENING HOURS

Most shops are open Monday to Friday 09.00–13.00 and
16.30–20.00 (or later in summer months), and on Saturday
mornings. The siesta is still a time-honoured custom in Palma and
very necessary during the hot summer months if you intend to keep
going into the small hours of the morning like the locals. The siesta
generally runs from 13.30 to as late as 17.00, although hypermarkets
and department stores remain open, as do many shops in the
coastal resorts. Restaurants don't normally start serving dinner until
20.00 and are at their busiest around 23.00, which is when the
discos and clubs start to fill up, although their special shows do not
normally begin until 01.00 or so.

Banks are generally open from Monday to Thursday 08.30–14.30,
and Fridays until 14.00. Most post offices open from Monday to
Friday from 09.30–13.00 and 16.00–19.00, and Saturday mornings,
but Palma's main post office in Carrer de Constitució is open
Monday to Friday from 08.30–20.30 and Saturdays from

09.30–14.00. Museum opening times vary. Most are open at least 10.00–13.00 and 16.00–18.00, and some have extended hours during summer. Many close for at least one day a week, often on Sunday or Monday.

TOILETS

Public toilets are still not widespread and it is no longer quite so common to wander into a bar merely to use their *servicios* without buying something. Indeed, many bars have notices prohibiting just that – you will see signs saying *Aseos reservados para clients* (lavatories reserved for clients only). Public toilets can be found in hypermarkets, supermarkets, department stores and underground car parks. However, they are unlikely to have paper. There are good facilities in all the major museums and galleries.

CHILDREN

Everyone is welcome in Palma, and children are no exception. In fact, they are often doted on. Restaurants, cafés and even bars will generally be happy to cater for children – many offer special children's menus or portions – and the preference for al fresco dining from April to October removes any concerns about smoky air and fidgeting.

If you need to hire a car seat for a child, double-check availability when making the booking and also check the seat carefully before fitting it. Nappies, baby food and formula milk can be bought in supermarkets in Palma, but if you have a preferred brand take a supply with you. Some hotels offer a room-listening service for the evenings. Ask your reception also about *canguros* (professional baby-sitters) and local *guarderías* (crèches).

The best local attractions for children are in the outskirts of

Palma or in the neighbouring coastal resorts. The following sights and activities are guaranteed to keep the kids entertained:

- **Boat trips** Around Palma Bay, from Passeig Marítim (see page 85). Some boats have glass bottoms so you can see the fish.

- **A hop-on-hop-off bus tour** (see page 56). Even the little ones enjoy getting on and off this open-top bus as it tours the city sights, and there's entertaining commentary on board for older children too.

- **A galeras ride** (see page 56). Explore Palma's old town by horse and carriage.

- **City parks** Check out the city's green spaces for football, picnics and fun on the swings, slides and climbing frames. The playground at the eastern end of Parc de la Mar is especially good for tinies.

- **Museu Munecas Antiguas** A tiny doll museum in Palma's old town. **ⓐ** Carrer Palau Real 27. **❶** 971 729850. **🕒** 10.00–18.00 Tues–Sun.

- **Coves de Gènova** (see page 100). A fascinating underground cavern complex.

- **The Palma-Sóller** Mountain train and tram (see page 128).

- **Festival Park** (see page 104). For cinemas, bowling, open-air entertainment and Europe's largest reptilarium.

- **Golf Fantasia** (see page 102). Minigolf for all the family in Palmanova, with three different courses set amid waterfalls, caves and tropical gardens.

- **Marineland, Costa d'En Blanes** (see page 104). A fantastic water park with displays of performing dolphins, sea lions and parrots.

● *A boat trip is a great treat for the kids*

- **Beaches and watersports** The fine sandy beaches at Cala Major, Portals Nous, Palmanova and Magaluf are all within easy reach of the city to the west, or head east to the Playa de Palma, 7 km (4 miles) of golden sandy beach stretching from Ca'n Pastilla to S'Arenal. As well as building sand castles and splashing about in the sea, each beach offers various watersports, from pedalo rides to more energetic activities for teenagers, such as windsurfing, canoeing and snorkelling.

- **Aqualand S'Arenal and Aqualand Magaluf** (see pages 104 and 106) – fantastic fun for all the family. Two giant waterparks with death-defying slides, thrilling rides for older kids, and some tamer ones for toddlers too.

- **Karting Magaluf** Older children in particular will enjoy racing around this go-kart track on the outskirts of Magaluf.

- **Western Water Park** Our mini-cowboys and Indians will love the horse-riding shows, the Indian battles and the can-can dancers. There are even water chutes and whirlpools for the adults.
  ⓐ Carretera Cala Figuera Sa Porrasa 12–22, Magaluf.
  ⓣ 971 131203. ⓦ www.westernpark.com ⓛ 10.00–18.00 May–Oct

COMMUNICATIONS
Phones
Public phones are easy to use. Most take coins, phone cards and credit cards and they have instructions for use in English: basically lift the receiver, insert payment and dial the number. Phone cards can be purchased from post offices and many other shops. Mallorca has a good mobile phone network, although you may have

problems getting a signal in parts of the interior. If you plan to use your mobile abroad, check with your service provider that you will be able to access the relevant networks.

To phone home from Palma, dial the international access code (00) followed by the relevant country code: UK 44, USA and Canada 1, Australia 61, New Zealand 64, Republic of Ireland 353, South Africa 72, then the local code (minus the initial 0, if there is one) and finally the number you want.

All telephone numbers in the Balearic Islands begin with 971 followed by a six-digit number. To call them from abroad, dial your international access code (00 in most countries), followed by the code for Spain (34), and then the number beginning with 971. The Mallorcan Yellow Pages (*Páginas Amarillas*) has a very comprehensive index in English. Its centre pages contain detailed street plans of Palma and other towns.

Calls to the operator ℹ️ 1002
International enquiries ℹ️ 11825
National enquiries ℹ️ 11818

Post

The Mallorcan post is moderately efficient. The bright yellow post offices and post boxes are easy to spot, and stamps (*sellos*) are available from any tobacconist or at the post office. The main post office in Palma is in Carrer de Constitució, and is open Mon–Fri 08.30–20.30, and Sat morning.

Internet cafés

The internet is a quick, cheap and easy way of keeping in touch while you are away, and cybercafés are currently popping up all over the city, including:

Xpace Internet Centre @ Carrer San Gaita 40. ☎ 971 729210.
🌐 www.xpacecyber.com 🕐 10.00–22.00 Mon–Sat, 14.00–22.00 Sun.

Manamú Café @ Carrer Concepció 5. ☎ 971 729294. 🕐 09.00–late
Mon–Fri, 19.00–late Sat.

Café Conectado @ Passeig de Mallorca 14. ☎ 971 714618.
🌐 www.café-conectado.com 🕐 08.30–22.30 Mon–Sat.

Blond Café @ Plaça Salvador Coll 10. ☎ 971 213646.
🌐 www.blondcafé.com 🕐 09.00–23.00 Mon–Sat (soon to be open
nightly until 03.00).

ELECTRICITY

Electricity is supplied at 220–225 volts. Spanish plugs are of the two-
pin round plug variety, so an adapter will be required for British and
non-Continental appliances. US and other visitors with 110-volt
appliances will need to use a voltage transformer, too. If you are
considering buying electrical appliances to take home, always check
that they will work in your home country before you buy.

TRAVELLERS WITH DISABILITIES

Although the authorities are working hard to improve facilities for
visitors with disabilities, much still remains to be done. Check with
your travel company on the hotels that provide facilities for the
disabled. All radio taxi companies offer modified taxis to
accommodate wheelchairs, but they need to be booked in advance.
For further information, contact:

Asprom Mallorca's main association for people with disabilities.
@ Carrer Pascual Ribot 6a. ☎ 971 289052.

Trip Scope Advice for UK-based travellers. ☎ 0845 758641.
🌐 www.tripscope.org.uk

Disabled Persons Transport Advisory Committee (UK)
Ⓦ www.dptac.gov.uk/door-to-door.
SATH (**Society for Accessible Travel & Hospitality**) advises US-based travellers with disabilities. ❸ 347 Fifth Ave, Suite 610, New York, NY 10016. ❶ (212) 447 7284. ❶ (212) 725 8253. Ⓦ www.sath.org.

FURTHER INFORMATION
Tourist Information Offices
Palma's Tourist Information Offices (*Oficines d'Informació Turística*) are useful for maps, attractions and event information and any other queries you have about the city. Two are located in the city centre and there is also one in Arrivals at the airport:
OIT Municipal de Palma ❸ Passeig des Born. ❶ 971 724090.
OIT Municipal de Palma ❸ Plaça d'Espanya ❶ 971 292758.
OIT Aeroport ❶ 971 789556.
Their official website is Ⓦ www.infomallorca.net

Further reading
Jogging around Majorca, Gordon West – a light-hearted account of island travels in the 1920s.
Problem at Pollensa Bay, Agatha Christie – a romantic short thriller set in the north-coast resort of Pollença.
Wild Olives, William Robert Graves – portraits of daily life in Mallorca with the English poet, novelist and former Deià resident, Robert Graves, written by his son.
Our Man in Majorca, Tom Crichton – an entertaining account of life as a tour rep in the 1960s.
Snowball Oranges and *Mañana Mañana*, Peter Kerr – an account of a Scottish family moving to Mallorca to run an orange farm, and its sequel, adjusting to the slow pace of island life.

Useful phrases

Although English is widely spoken in Palma, these words and phrases may come in handy. See also the phrases for specific situations in other parts of the book.

English	Spanish	Approx. pronunciation
BASICS		
Yes	Sí	Si
No	No	Noh
Please	Por favor	Por fabor
Thank you	Gracias	Gratheeas
Hello	Hola	Ola
Goodbye	Adiós	Adeeos
Excuse me	Disculpe	Deeskoolpeh
Sorry	Perdón	Pairdohn
That's okay	De acuerdo	Dey acwerdo
To	A	A
From	Desde/de	Desdey/dey
I don't speak Spanish	No hablo español	Noh ahblo espanyol
Do you speak English?	¿Habla usted inglés?	¿Ahbla oosteth eengless?
Good morning	Buenos días	Bwenos dee-ahs
Good afternoon	Buenas tardes	Bwenas tarrdess
Good evening	Buenas noches	Bwenas notchess
Goodnight	Buenas noches	Bwenas notchess
My name is ...	Me llamo ...	Meh lliamo ...
DAYS & TIMES		
Monday	Lunes	Loones
Tuesday	Martes	Martes
Wednesday	Miércoles	Meeyercoles
Thursday	Jueves	Hooebes
Friday	Viernes	Beeyernes
Saturday	Sábado	Sabadoe
Sunday	Domingo	Domeengo
Morning	Mañana	Manyana
Afternoon	Tarde	Tardey
Evening	Noche	Nochey
Night	Noche	Nochey
Yesterday	Ayer	Ayer

English	Spanish	*Approx. pronunciation*
Today	Hoy	*Oy*
Tomorrow	Mañana	*Manyana*
What time is it?	¿Qué hora es?	*¿Kay ora es?*
It is ...	Son las ...	*Son las ...*
09.00	Nueve	*Nwebey*
Midday	Mediodía	*Medeeodeea*
Midnight	Medianoche	*Medeeanoche*

NUMBERS

One	Uno	*Oono*
Two	Dos	*Dos*
Three	Tres	*Tres*
Four	Cuatro	*Cwatro*
Five	Cinco	*Thinco*
Six	Seis	*Seys*
Seven	Siete	*Seeyetey*
Eight	Ocho	*Ocho*
Nine	Nueve	*Nwebey*
Ten	Diez	*Deeyeth*
Eleven	Once	*Onthey*
Twelve	Doce	*Dothey*
Twenty	Veinte	*Beintey*
Fifty	Cincuenta	*Thincwenta*
One hundred	Cien	*Thien*

MONEY

I would like to change these traveller's cheques/this currency	Quisiera cambiar estos cheques de viaje/dinero	*Keyseeeyera canbeear estos chekes de beeahe/denero*
Where is the nearest ATM?	¿Dónde está el cajero automático más cercano?	*¿Dondeh estah el cakhehroh der beeyeh ler plew prosh?*
Do you accept credit cards?	¿Aceptan tarjetas de crédito?	*¿Atheptan tarhetas deh credeeto?*

SIGNS & NOTICES

Airport	Aeropuerto	*Aehropwerto*
Rail station/Platform	Estación de trenes/Vía	*Estatheeon de tren/Veea*
Smoking/non-smoking	Fumadores/No fumadores	*Foomadoores/no foomadoores*
Toilets	Servicios	*Serbeetheeos*
Ladies/Gentlemen	Señoras/Caballeros	*Senyoras/Kaballieros*
Subway	Metro	*Metro*

155

Emergencies

EMERGENCY NUMBERS

Emergency Coordination Centre 112 (dial this number in any type of emergency. They speak English and will alert the relevant service).
Police (Policía Nacional, for theft) 091 (Palma) or 112 (rest of island).
City Police (Policia Municipal, for traffic accidents) 092 (Palma) or 112 (rest of island).
Fire (Bomberos) 080 (Palma); 085 (rest of the island).
Ambulance (Ambulància) 112.
General medical emergencies 061.
Private medical assistance (24 hour) 900 722222.

MEDICAL EMERGENCIES

Should you become seriously ill, lists of local doctors, dentists and hospitals can be found in telephone directories, local newspapers or by contacting your consulate, who have lists of English-speaking practitioners. Alternatively, ask your hotel reception to help, or, in a real emergency, dial 112. If you have a valid European Health Insurance Card (EHIC, see page 145), you should ensure that the doctor is part of the Spanish healthcare system, as the card only covers state-provided medical treatment. Be forewarned; it may not cover all the things you may expect to receive free of charge. If you are seen at a private clinic, you will need to pay on the spot and be reimbursed by your insurance company at a later date.

In an emergency, go to the Outpatient emergency department of Hospital Son Dureta, the university hospital, which is located on the outskirts of the city, just north of Castell de Bellver.

Hospital Son Dureta 🅰 Carrer Andrea Dòria 55. ☎ 971 175500
🚌 Bus 4 or 5.

POLICE STATIONS

Police stations are open 24 hours a day.

Policia Municipal ⓐ Carrer de Sant Ferran, Palma. ⓣ 971 225500.

Policia Nacional ⓐ Carrer de Ruiz Alda 8, Palma. ⓣ 971 225200.

LOST PROPERTY

Lost property should be reported to the local police station, even if only for insurance purposes. If found, it should end up at the town hall ⓐ Plaça Cort 1. ⓣ 971 225900. Report lost passports to your Consulate.

Embassies and consulates

UK ⓐ Avinguda Plaça Major 3D, Palma. ⓣ 971 712085.

United States ⓐ Carrer Porto Pi, 8, Palma. ⓣ 971 403707.

Canadian ⓐ Plaça de Catalunya 9, Barcelona. ⓣ 93 4127236

Australian ⓐ Plaza del Descubridor Diego de Ordas 3, Madrid. ⓣ 91 3536600.

New Zealand ⓐ 3rd floor, Plaza de La Lealtad 2, Madrid. ⓣ 91 5230226.

South African ⓐ Parc Empresarial Mas Blau II, Alta Ribagorza 6–8, Prat de Llobregar, Barcelona. ⓣ 935 069100

EMERGENCY PHRASES

Help! ¡Socorro! *¡Sawkoro!*   **Fire!** ¡Fuego! *¡Fwegoh!*

Stop! ¡Stop! *¡Stop!*

Call an ambulance/a doctor/the police/the fire service!
¡Llame a una ambulancia/un médico/la policía/a los bomberos!
¡Lliame a oona anboolanthea/oon meydico/la poletheea/a lohs bombehrohs!

The publishers would like to thank the following individuals and organisations for supplying their copyright photographs for this book.

A1 Pix: pages 5, 7, 67, 68, 101, 103, 129, 131, 136, 138/139, 141 & 149
Iberimage: pages 11 & 45
Hotel Palau Sa Font: page 35
Hotel Valparaíso Palace: page 37
Teresa Fisher: all other pages.

Proofreader: Jan McCann
Copy-editor: Stephen York

Send your thoughts to
books@thomascook.com

- Found a great bar, club, shop or must-see sight that we don't feature?

- Like to tip us off about any information that needs a little updating?

- Want to tell us what you love about this handy little guidebook and more importantly how we can make it even handier?

Then here's your chance to tell all! Send us ideas, discoveries and recommendations today and then look out for your valuable input in the next edition of this title. As an extra 'thank you' from Thomas Cook Publishing, you'll be automatically entered into our exciting monthly prize draw.

Email the above address (stating the book's title) or write to: CitySpots Project Editor, Thomas Cook Publishing, PO Box 227, Unit 15/16, Coningsby Road, Peterborough PE3 8SB, UK.